[COPY.]

EWHURST PARK,

BASINGSTOKE,

9 April, 1909.

DEAR MR. CLIFT,

I sent a copy of your book to an old friend of mine, a very able man and for many years a Professor of Glasgow University. I do not send you his letter because his handwriting is so bad I think you would have a difficulty in making out what he says, but I am copying that part of his letter which refers to the book and which I thought would interest you. He says "I am perfectly delighted with the book. I have read every word of it with the greatest interest and read out various things in it to my wife. Mr. Clift is a splendid fellow—something *like* an Englishman. He gives one a picture of what an English farmer's life is, what farming means, whence come failure and success, such as I have never seen so graphically put before. Self help and good character are the foundation of success in farming as in everything else—a plain truth utterly forgotten by your would-be reformers of to-day. There are all sorts of interesting things and no end of funny information in the Reminiscences, and no end of wisdom. It has been quite a treat to read it, and I send you my best thanks for sending it me." I sent him a copy without any comment just to see what his opinion would be and I fully agree with every word of it.

Yours sincerely,

WELLINGTON.

The Reminiscences of

William Clift,

of Bramley,

Born 1828 and wrote these my

Reminiscences 1908.

Dedicated to

his Grace the Duke of Wellington, K.G.

(By Permission),

A Son of the Soil,
With health and contentment,
The result of my toil.

INTRODUCTION.

To sit down and write out what one can remember of one's life, trying to recall events that have come about, during a period of seventy-five or more years, as part of that life, is not, I feel, a small matter to undertake. But as I have hours on hand which I can very well give to the purpose, I shall try to bring to mind what I can of the people whom I have known in the course of my life, and of the places in which they lived.

In talking to a gentleman a short time ago, he suggested, at the close of our conversation, that if I could put on paper similar recollections to those I had just told him of, many persons would be glad to gather them together, and make a book of them.

So I commenced to see what I could do, and here I set it down.   W.C.

THE REMINISCENCES OF WILLIAM CLIFT.

CHAPTER I.

THE CLIFTS AT BRAMLEY.

My father was fifth in descent from John Clift, who came into Bramley in 1673, and took Hyde House Farm. He was Overseer of Bramley 1673-6. My father was second son of my grandfather, William Clift, and was born at Stocks Farm (where I now live) in 1782. (From a map of Stocks Farm, 1762, when occupied by my great-grandfather, my family appear to have owned, as well as occupied, land in Bramley. These holdings must have been sold in my uncle Joseph's time. The said Joseph Clift, being my grandfather's heir, took the land on the death of my grandfather, who left no will.) My father married, in 1811, Ann Bennett, of Minchen's Farm, in Bramley, and went into business at Oliver's Farm, also in Bramley. He held this farm only one year, and then came to Hollow Cross, which he took of his cousin, William Clift, who died at Stoken Church, Oxon, in 1833, and was buried here at Bramley. On the death of my father's cousin William (the owner of Hollow Cross), his son Jesse became my father's landlord. He willed that the farm should be sold, at his death, on condition that my father be still allowed to rent it. It was offered to the Duke of Wellington, and he bought it for £1200, and it has been held by us uninterruptedly since that time. I took it of the Duke in 1874, after it was given up by my two brothers, Thomas and Daniel. My desire was to keep it in the family. My father lived the rest of his life at Hollow Cross, dying in 1855. He also occupied, after John Bennett's death, Minchen's Farm. My father left Minchen's Farm in 1835, and took Barefoot's and Hyde House Farms, owned by the Fanshawe family of Eastbourne. Admiral Fanshawe sold the farms to the Duke of Wellington, who thus bought all the farms during the occupation of them by my father. My mother died in 1836, on September 30th, leaving ten living children (six sons and four daughters), of whom I am the fifth surviving son, and as far as I can trace from the register I am the fifth William Clift that has resided at the Stocks out of six tenants of the Clift family. My uncle, Jesse Clift, followed on after the death of my

grandfather, William Clift, who died in 1818. He
left a son William, but he was a printer, and
lived at Cirencester, Gloucestershire. It has so
happened that I am the fifth son of my father out
of the ten children he reared, and fifth in descent from
the first William that lived here. It is curious that
the same Christian and surname should have been re-
instated in the same place unforeseen, unpremeditated,
entirely by the good fortune of my coming to take
up my employment as overlooker of the Beaurepaire
Estate, under kind Mrs. Brocas, whose name I
greatly revere and think of with much pleasure and
thankfulness. Her kindness was not derived from
what she saw of me, as, I am sorry to say, her
sight had entirely left her before I knew her. My
ancestors seem to have taken great interest in Church
matters from the very first of their coming into
the parish. The first William held a record of
years as Churchwarden from 1686 to 1710—a
period of twenty-four years, and other callings such
as ringer and singer. I suppose I might claim
for myself the record for church choir singers, which
is now seventy years. I was also a church ringer
part of the time.

CHAPTER II.

MY BOYHOOD AT BRAMLEY.

One of the first things I can remember in my childhood is the funeral of my father's cousin, William Clift, the owner of Hollow Cross Farm. I can remember the hearse rested on the Green outside Hollow Cross, the body having been conveyed from Stoken Church in Oxfordshire for burial at Bramley.

I went to a school at Fair Oak, Stratfieldsaye, which Mrs. Lavington kept. Ten of us Clifts, with eleven of Farmer Fabery's children, attended the school as we got old enough. Mrs. Lavington combined three businesses—school-keeping, smock-frock making, and on Saturdays she acted as public carrier to Reading. Her husband rented a few meadows, and had been, I believe, a small farmer, so called in those days. The cultivation of land seemed the principal occupation for getting a livelihood at that time. Many a tale could I tell of those schooldays. Mrs. Lavington pursued her work of smock-making while teaching (or supposed to be teaching) us. She had a long pair of scissors tied to her apron string on her side, and with them used to point out the letters to us. We used to sit upon little open forms round the room. One boy could not say the letter W, but used to call it bubbycoo, and this caused a little giggling amongst the others. When we behaved badly she would fling her cane at us, and make the boy she considered the worst bring it back to her, and if he did not draw back his hand pretty quickly, he would get a stroke as a receipt for him to keep it in mind.

I must say a word about the smock-frocks old Dame Lavington made. They were made reversible so that they could be turned. They were supposed to be worn one day one side to the front, and the next day the other, so that they might be worn alike, and last longer.

Our games were simple enough. "Puss wants a corner" was often played. Three willow pollards stood outside the school. Each pollard was a "corner" and was taken each by a boy, while a fourth boy, carrying a ball, wandered about crying "Poor puss wants a corner." The three boys at the corners had to keep changing their places; and if, while changing, the boy with the ball could throw at and hit either of them, the boy so hit had to become "Puss" in his turn.

We used to find diversion sometimes in playing various tricks on those around us. Tailor Cane's long pipe, which he would smoke down the road in going from his house to his farm, and then hide in a hollow pollard, while he went to see to his little farm at the corner of Mill Lane and Folly Lane, was often missing when he returned. Our fun was to see him search for it.

Joe Godden (or Smith, as he was sometimes called) who kept the "Fighting Cocks" near by, afforded us occasionally much amusement. He would relate his experiences at the Duke's house when he went to measure the Marquis of Douro and Lord Charles Wellesley for their shoes. They would not get out of bed to let old Joe measure them properly, but poked their feet from under the clothes, and played all sorts of pranks with him whilst he was doing it. When we annoyed Joe, as we often did beyond his patience, he would go out to his shop door and call "Books! Books!" to make us believe it was Mrs. Lavington, who used to do this when it was time for us to go back to school, so that we might leave him in peace; but we used to try and leave a little dab of his shoemaker's wax on his seat, if we could, for him to sit on when he went back. Joe Pocock, the thresher, used to get us to fetch his dinner beer from the "Fighting Cocks," and take to him where he worked in Tailor Cane's barn at thrashing, the reward being a half-penny. Sometimes it was dropped among the straw to puzzle us to find it.

About the year 1836, or soon after, I went to the Duke's School at Stratfieldsaye, under Daniel Sweetzer. The Duke paid the schooling of his own tenants' children in the parish, but we being out of the parish, had to pay 8d. per week.

About this time the singing broke down in Stratfieldsaye Church, and the Great Duke had his school-children taught the tonic sol-fa, to enable them to be in the choir at church. Our singing - teacher was a lady from Mr. Binfield's music shop at Reading. At this time they had a barrel-organ in the church, which is still there, but unused.

I remember well the Rector bringing the Duke to the school to hear the children sing their exercises. Although I did not belong to the parish, I was asked to join them in singing. At first, when we were called up to sing, his presence made our "do re mi" rather shaky, so I thought it should not be so with me next time. When it came to my turn to sing, I stepped forward, and sang louder and better, and the Duke said, in a deep voice, "Very good, very good."

The Rector, the Rev. Gerald Wellesley, was often seen by us as he went about the parish visiting his parishioners, to whom he was very benevolent. He used to ask me to go to his church on Sundays. To me he was most kind. He used to tell me to go to the Rectory for all that I wanted on Sundays when I went to his church to help the choir. Numberless tales might be told of the Rector's benevolence, which was shrewdly bestowed. Here is a sample. He was in the habit, when visiting the cottagers, of asking what they were in need of. One cottager, so asked, replied, "Please, sir, my husband is bad off for shoes." "Well," said the Rector, "go to Joe Godden's, and get you a pair for him : you pay for one, and I'll pay for the other. I'll let him know that when you pay for your shoe he is to give you the pair."

One incident comes vividly to my mind which occurred when playing one of our schoolboy tricks. The road-man, Welch, was nick-named "Fuddle" by the boys on account of his drinking habits. We used to cause him great annoyance by so addressing him. One morning we thought that we would arouse his anger, so we all began by calling him "Fuddle" as we passed him on our way to school, for we had to pass him as he was working on the road. We agreed to go in singly, at safe intervals, and each boy, when he had passed him, was to call him by his hated nick-name, Fuddle. But his anger reached such a pitch that before the unfortunate last boy could get out of reach, he flung his spade at him and knocked him down flat on the ground.

In 1838 I went to the Vyne with other children from this parish to be inoculated for the small pox. Mrs. Chute performed the operation with a silver lance. I fancy I can even now see the raisins placed on a long table to be given to the children to keep them from crying and as a reward for submitting to it.

The winter of 1838 was very severe. It was called "Murphy's winter" from its prognosticator, one Murphy. There was thirteen weeks' frost, from Christmas to the end of March. We heard of the roasting of an ox on the Thames in London. The higher class people were unable to travel about on wheel vehicles, so they used sledges to slide along on the top of the snow, which was very slippery. The sledge was made very light so that the horse could travel along at a good pace. Nearly all the farmers' teams went to the chalk pits for chalk almost every day, and much of the land got chalked that year.

CHAPTER III.

MY WORK AS A LAD AT HOME.

When I left school, my work was to look after the pigs, cows, and pony. Our time for rising was 4.30 in the summer, and shortly after 5 in winter. Before breakfast we had all the cattle to feed ; and after breakfast (which we took at 6 in the summer, and about 6.30 in the winter) we started, with the carters, to our work for the day. We had breakfast by candle light, or, I might say, rushlight, in winter. My father knew how to make his rushlight for economy's sake. It is a pleasant recollection, the economical ways of the past.

Our cows, five or six in number, were kept for the fattening of calves, or "suckling." Our system was this : The young calf lay with its mother for two days, when born ; then it was put away to lie loose for about a fortnight. Then a halter and chain were put on it, and it was tied up to the end of a trough, in which was placed dry pounded chalk for it to lick at its leisure. The chalk was pounded in a box by a mallet : this was done regularly once a day while the calves were suckling, in the morning generally. In the afternoon a bundle of clean wheat straw was fetched in for their litter : this being regularly done, they were kept quite clean. The chalk was given them that the flesh should look white (we called veal "white meat"). We used to keep about three calves to two cows ; by careful management sometimes the proportion was more. I believe the cows were made to pay very well. I well remember that one cow ("Old Peg" I used to call her) was very subject to sore teats, sometimes due to the drying on them of the froth made by the calf when sucking. This caused the teats to chap and become so tender that it was often difficult to get her to let the calf suck. So I thought I would try to remedy this by regularly washing the udder with cold spring water. This, done morning and night for three successive days, quite cured it ; and to this day my remedy for chaps or sores is bathing freely in cold spring water, or tying on wet rags and frequently wetting them with cold water.

I had to take these cows up into Hyde House pastures ; and the way to get there was up old Hyde House Lane. It was so bad that I could not myself go up it, but was obliged to go over into the field, getting the cows along by whacking sticks and clumpets and hallooing over the hedge at them. The process of moving these old cows was so slow that I thought I would try a fresh plan to get them along faster. I began to train one of them to carry me on her back down the lane and drive the others before me. This feat I achieved by scratching her at the root of the tail or in the poll. It is very soothing to a cow to scratch her in either of these places, and the cow would stretch out her neck and put out her tongue as far as she could get it, to show her appreciation. Her enjoyment of it was so great that she would try and do it herself when I left off. The cow soon became tame enough to let me get on her back and drive the others before me with a whip in my hand to the pasture through the muddy lane.

On another occasion I tried another manœuvre to save myself trouble. I taught my dog to fetch the cows up to the gate for me. On dark mornings, as soon as I got up, which was about half-past five, the dog was sent off ; and by the time I was ready to start off, he would have the cows at the gate waiting for me, so that I had only to open the gate and bring them home. This, of course, helped forward my morning's work.

When I became big enough to take up regular work on the farm, I may fairly say that I did so with interest : I always tried to do what I took in hand as well as other people, who were older than I, did theirs. Whenever opportunity occurred, I tried to learn any new thing. I suppose I thought myself very mannish, and would try to do my work as the men. When I went to harrow in wheat-sowing time (which was one of the jobs a boy was set to do when he first started work) I sometimes tried my hand at sowing. If the seedsman put his seedlip down, and if I could get his back turned for a little while, I would get hold of the seedlip and sow a land, putting a mark in the hedge opposite where I began and ended, and afterwards comparing mine with the other corn when it came up side by side.

This is how a typical day at that time of my life was passed. Out early in the field, we set to work till luncheon time. My two eldest brothers, Thomas and Daniel, were the two carters, John was seedsman, and I harrow-boy. It was our general practice to have our luncheon in the field when out with the horses. It usually consisted of bread and cheese, with small beer, which was brewed at home specially for that purpose, and which we carried to the field in wooden bottles. We always drank from a wooden bottle, first the carters and then the boys. 'Twas much enjoyed in this fashion. A piece of good hay was laid down to each horse for his lunch at the same time, and I think horses, men, and boys, seemed alike to enjoy the rest and refreshment. We used to stop from twenty minutes to half-an-hour for luncheon, never more. Then on to work

"The birds they sang, and so did we,
    With a pop of the whip and gee up gee,"

till three o'clock, when the teams "shot off," except the harrow boy's team, which was left behind the others to finish up the day's work properly. The year 1844 was a very wet year. The seed was sown quickly after the plough, and it required a deal of harrowing behind. But I remember the year following, 1845 : it was an excellent wheat crop, with scarcely any weed in it. Heavy seasons were always considered the best for growing a crop of wheat. I thought mine was the hardest job in the field : I had to keep my harrows clean, and stay after the others had gone home to finish the work up all close. Furrows had to be struck and made clear for the water to get off in case there came a shower in the night, and old Abraham Wheeler, and perhaps Tom Leadbetter, had the job to keep them clear when once they were made.

So the time passed on until I was able to take to any kind of work on the farm. While working as a boy in the fields I had ample opportunities for observing things ; and I can recall many instances where my observations of the habits and peculiarities of the animals and birds, which at the time seemed very trifling and frivolous, but have since stood me in good stead. The ways of them all interested me at the time, and often I had much to think of in my leisure moments about what I had seen. Sometimes I learnt of myself, and sometimes others pointed out to me things which I might otherwise have missed. For instance, I remember a lesson about the power of the human eye. I was taking my father's sheep into the field, and they ran off along the wrong road. Tom Leadbetter, a boy, was near, so I asked him to run past them and stop them. For some time he could not overtake them ; but they stopped, and he got past them. When he got back, I asked him how he managed to get by them. "Oh," said Tom, "when they stopped I just 'shut my eyes' and slipped by them." I had a hearty laugh at Tom's ideas, but afterwards thought there was something in it. Reasoning that it must be the eye of human beings which animals fear, I tried it on after this with a blackbird. In the hedge in the old green lane leading from Barefoot's Farm to Stratfieldsaye I found a blackbird's nest, on which the old bird was sitting. Having passed her quietly several mornings, I thought I would try to catch her on the nest. I put my hand behind me so that I could take her off as soon as I touched her, and slowly walked backwards to her nest, took her off quietly, and carried her home and put her into a cage. I accomplished this by keeping the sight of my eyes from her.

I remember seeing one day, in that same green lane, a covey of partridges, ten in number, running before me. They ran into a big bush. Thought I to myself, "If they stay there long enough for me to get near, I will have a throw at them." Nine of them got up before I got near enough to throw, but as I had counted them in and out, I knew there was one left in the bush. I had an apple and a pear in my pocket, and, boy-like, I hardly knew which I would sooner lose, but I decided to throw the pear. When I got near enough I gave the bush a kick, and up got the bird. When about twelve to eighteen yards away and four or five feet from the ground, I threw the pear with my left hand and fetched down the partridge as clean as the best of shots. I picked it up, took it home, and gave it to my uncle Thomas, but I don't remember having a sixpence for it, which was rather disappointing. I have taken many a bird off the limb of a tree by my left-handed throw, but remember only this one pulled down when on the wing.

So my life as a boy was not all hard work and no play. We used sometimes to watch the sport when shooting time came. Before the Duke bought the Barefoots and Hollow Cross Farms a Mr. Henry Randall used to shoot over them. He was, I believe, a barrister by profession, and being particularly nice and gentlemanly we, as boys, were always pleased to see him. As his groom did not always come with him, we were always ready to offer our services to take his horse out and so on. He would ask to have his lunch brought out to him in such and such a field at one o'clock. I generally looked out to get the job if I could. Once when I took his lunch up I asked him if he was having good sport. "Oh, yes!" said he, "I have just killed a hare—as fine a hare as ever was 'filled'"—an expression I had never heard before. I used to wait for him until he had done his lunch, when I took the basket and what game he had to his trap for him, while he stopped and took a few sips out of his silver flask. When about to start home it was his custom to take out a long knitted purse from his pocket. Gentlemen carried such purses then. They had two compartments divided by two silver rings. I know that, boy-like, I concluded that the knob at one end must be silver, and that the other nice little knob must be gold. I used to watch keenly the process of opening this purse. One ring was slacked, a shilling taken out and given to me. You may imagine how quickly my hand went to my cap with a "Thank you, Sir!" His gun was an object of curiosity to us. We used to think what a nice gun it was. After using it was always taken to pieces, wiped clean, and put into a case. It was fired off with percussion caps, which were then new to us. Our own guns were of the old flint-and-steel pattern, in which the lock was furnished with a pan holding a little loose powder, which was covered by a piece of steel. A piece of flint was fastened into the hammer by a screw. When the trigger was pulled it struck against the steel and produced a spark, which ignited the powder, causing the gun to go off. When the powder was damp it often misfired. The powder would "fizz" a little while, and then go off "bang!" It required a good shot to pull down a bird when this happened. I had once in my hand a double-barrelled flint gun which was used by my uncle, Thomas Davis, for game shooting. He was a noted man with his gun, but like many others I have known in my time, it got him into trouble. He had to leave his farm and take a gamekeeper's situation, and ended his days a servant instead of a master. Three of his sons, who were excellent and steady men, also became gamekeepers and did well. I believe one took out no less than fifty-six game certificates under one employer. This same Thomas Davis was as I have been told, once out on Barefoot's Farm with his gun. A covey of ten partridges got up and flew between two willow pollards [still standing] at the top of "Fourteen-acres" field [so called at the present time]. He fired just as they were flying between the trees, and picked up nine of the ten as the result of his shot.

An Old Winnowing Fan and Shovel.

CHAPTER IV.

TAKING THE CORN TO MARKET.

When I was a lad at home my brother Thomas had to take the corn to Reading market on Saturdays, from Michaelmas to Christmas; the best team had to go with a "carriage" of corn (that is, a four-horse load of ten or twelve quarters). My brother used to get his food put up on Friday, ready for Saturday; it was packed in a large basket. On Friday night the waggon was loaded, drawn out, and clothed down; care being taken to leave the waggon on a good piece of ground, so that they might have a good start. At about 12 o'clock midnight they began their journey, reaching Reading about six in the morning. I believe the carters used to take most of the harness off, on arrival, and clean their horses down, and feed them, just as they would in the morning at home. This refreshed the horses.

A sample sack of wheat was taken out of the waggon, and carried up into the Market Place, for the salesman to sell the bulk by. When sold, the carter was told to "draw away," that is, take it to the buyer's granary. As soon as delivery was made, the buyer was expected to pay for the corn, at the agreed price.

This done, the carters got ready for their journey

home. They generally started from Reading about 2 p.m., reaching home about 5 o'clock. As soon as they reached home, the horses were "shot out," and well attended to : we youngsters willingly helping, and making all sorts of enquiries as to what the carters had done and seen in Reading.

The carters took great pride in their teams. The horses' tails were neatly plaited down, and tied up with braid of various colours, making them look very smart. My brother's team used generally to wear "latten" bells, which father had bought for himself when he went with his father's horses. A team, going away from home, was not reckoned in first-class style unless furnished with bells. The bells were fixed in iron frames by leather hoops, and the frames were fixed to the two hames of the horse. The "fore'st" (foremost or first) horse and the "lash" (second) horse, had four bells each. The "body" (third) and the "thiller" (fourth) horses had three each. Each set of bells was tuned harmoniously ; of the set of three, for instance, the middle bell was larger than either of the others ; and three different tones were produced. The sets themselves varied in size also ; the first horse carried the smallest bells, while the fourth carried the largest. So that when in motion, the team announced its presence by a variety of musical sounds. I know we, as youngsters, would listen for them on their return from Reading ; and on hearing the faint tinkle in the distance, rush indoors with the welcome news that they were within hearing. It was called ten miles to Reading.

From Bramley, four-horse teams, with waggon loads of hops, used to go to Weyhill Fair on October 10th. Hops were then grown in this parish. In my grandfather's time there were several hop gardens on this farm which are marked on a map I have dated 1762—one field at the back of Stocks Farm leading into the rick-yard, and one next the meadow of the same farm on the road leading to Sherfield. These fields still go in the name of the Old Hop Gardens. I believe this to be the reason why the farmers invested their savings in plots of land, because it was very remunerative growing hops at that time. There was also a hop garden in Minchin's Lane, leading to Cluit's Green. There were also four hop kilns in the parish at one time and another—one near the Church, one on the Stratfieldsaye road, one at Stocks Farm, and another in Bramley Street. The one on the Stratfieldsaye road belonged to my father's uncle for his Hollow Cross Farm. These hop waggon teams, like our own teams, carried bells, but theirs were "rumblers" (so called)— round bells with a loose, rolling ball like a marble inside. At Stocks Farm one of the sets of old leather-covered bell-frames is still to be seen complete for the four horses.

CHAPTER V.

BRAMLEY IN THE OLD DAYS.

In the old days the Bramley labourers wore green smocks on week-days and white ones, to go to Church in, on Sundays. I think the wearing of white smocks was peculiar to our village, for they were called as a jest "the Bramley livery." The labourers attended Church regularly, and would walk home in groups discussing the sermon. The afternoon service, which was without sermon, was also well attended. The dress generally worn with the green smock was cord breeches and leather or fustian leggings. Afterwards "bettermost" people took to kerseymere. This was the time when

"Buckskin breeches were all the wear,
But now 'tis turned to Kerseymere"

was then a common saying.

The women went to Church in pattens. These pattens they were so used to that they would walk to Basingstoke and back on them. We have one woman still living in the parish (Jane Bartlett, 88 years of age) who, the other day, told me that, in her younger days, she once walked from Bramley to Maidenhead (over 20 miles) in one day on pattens.

The "Bramley Lanes," dear to Miss Mitford, were but green lanes till 1830, when the roads from Stratfieldsaye, by Hollow Cross, to where the station now is, and from Sherfield, over Bow Bridge, to the same spot, and from thence through Bramley to Sherborne and Pamber, were made. When there were only green lanes, foot-people walked inside the fields on the footpaths, it being impossible for them to get along the lanes, in which only strong carts and waggons could be used. The cart I remember my father used to ride to market in was called a shay cart, which was a body put on a pair of wheels without any springs under it. The shafts had iron loops on the end to put another horse on to help them out of the ruts. Before this, no one could come into Bramley without fording a stream. Bow Bridge, over the mouth of the Little Loddon, which joins the Loddon proper in Boar Mead in Sherfield, was the first bridge built. When this bridge was removed, and a new one was made, in 1903, the date 1830 was found inscribed on one of the bricks. Next came Locksbridge, built only a few years ago, where the parish was entered from Basing. Then Beaurepaire Mill Bridge, built in 1831, bearing the Brocas coat-of-arms, with date, upon it. It was built when the new road was made from Bramley Street, through Pepper Wood, on to Pamber (the Basingstoke and Aldermaston turnpike). This road was made the boundary to the Vyne and Beaurepaire Estates, exchanges being made of the straggling fields. As a proof of the bad state of the roads before they were macadamized, I may mention that I've read in the parish magazine of Mortimer, written by the

Rector there, that Mrs. Harriet Brocas, who used to live at Wokefield and sometimes at Beaurepaire, and who died in 1819, when she wanted to go from one house to the other, the journey took her the best part of a day to do it; and I've been told that she used to drive four black horses, and then could only go at foot pace, with two men walking by the side carrying poles with which they could help the wheels out of the deep ruts from time to time. Next Boar's Bridge was made, which marks the boundary of Bramley and Pamber. All these bridges are over the Little Loddon, which joins the Loddon proper at Sherfield. The Little Loddon (as I have called it) takes its rise somewhere in Pamber Forest, and comes along at the foot of the hill at Little London (so called), which, I believe, should be Little *Loddon* (not London), taking its name originally from the stream. The stream is a boundary mark, parting Sherborne St. John from Bramley, through the Beaurepaire Park Estate; then dividing Basing from Bramley, and Sherfield from Bramley.

There are three approaches to Bramley from Silchester, two of which were improved by bridges— at Latchmere Green and near the Bungalow. One bridge was built by the then Squire Brocas, and another one over the Little Loddon in Beaurepaire Park, as the family used to reside a good deal at that time at these two houses, and had very heavy goods to shift from Wokefield to Beaurepaire. I have been told that the large iron gates at the entrance over the moat leading up to Beaurepaire House were brought from Wokefield. I can well remember when this bridge was built. The timber they used for it was cut down on my father's farm. The third road is still through a ford at Clappers Farm. This stream also rises in Pamber Forest, and flows through Mortimer, Grazeley, and the lower end of Shinfield into the Kennett. Stratfieldsaye had two entrances to Bramley —one through the brook below Hollow Cross, and again through the same brook in Folly Lane. Farmer Fabery made the roads, and was for that reason nicknamed "Macadam." The gravel was brought from Silchester and Heckfield, and each tenant helped to draw it, the number of loads being according to the size of his farm — twenty yards to one hundred acres.

When I was a lad, James Gosling kept the "Three Pigeons" beerhouse, and was also a shoe-maker and preacher. On Sundays he combined preaching with beer-selling, opening his premises from two o'clock to three for business purposes, and from three to five o'clock to hold a religious service. He was accounted good at expounding the Scriptures.

Olive Sweetzer, "the Whisperer," was most notable for her skill in nursing the women of the parish in child-birth. I believe she nursed my mother with most of her children. She used to "whisper" away gathered fingers and other such diseases, and when anyone had the misfortune to run a thorn into their hand or finger they went to Olive

Sweetzer to have it "whispered." Her custom was to wet her longest finger on her tongue, rub the place over with it, and whisper, but what she whispered the patient must not know, or the charm would have no effect. I was told that my uncle Jesse ran a thorn through his finger and went to her and she quite cured it.

Sally Griggs, a noted straw-plaiter, lived at Hide House. She made up the plait into high-crowned hats for men. Straw-plaiting was practised in several cottages in Bramley; one was at Lone Barn. Three kinds of plait were made—seven-straw, five-straw, and knot-plait.

Old Dame Godden, or "Peggy," as she was more often called, another notable woman, lived just outside Bramley, at a place called "Smoky Hole," on the footpath leading from Bramley to Basingstoke. The people called her notable because she "could do five things at once." She could

Sit, and read, knit and smoke,
And show a man the way to Basingstoke.

She was a famous straw-plaiter and hat-maker. She could, if required, make hats of any style. She was particularly good at making the hats with tall crowns—similar in shape to the dress hats of that period, which were made of beaver. Hats of that shape are now made of silk, and are much lighter than the old beaver hats.

Mrs. Sam Tubb, of Sherfield Farm, was noted

for her ointment, which was in great request for curing all kinds of sores.

Old Mrs. Pink, of Bramley Green, was notable for her distilled essences of peppermint and other herbs.

Of the farms in Bramley at that time, Minchin's, which was owned by the Beaurepaire Estate, and was occupied by my father, and Hollow Cross was tenanted and owned by William Clift, my father's cousin.

Barefoot's Farm was held by Tom Davis, who married my father's eldest sister. After him came T. and W. Godden, and a few years afterwards the farm came into my father's hands.

Folly Farm was tenanted by two brothers, Joel and Charles Staniford. Charles walked in his sleep, and it was said that in his sleep one night he got up, went to the stable and gave the horses some hay out of the loft, and woke as he was coming down the ladder.

Lily Mill had two brothers as tenants, named Godden, who afterwards went to Barefoot's. Then Thomas Matthews took Lily Mill, and his son followed him. The old house stood near where the mill now stands, but the Great Duke pulled it down, and built the present house on a new piece of ground, and cut a road straight to Sherfield, by the Mill. Mr. Butler, from Wiltshire, succeeded the younger Matthews.

Bramley Green Farm was held by William Butler, who was followed by his son William. The first was a shoemaker. He married the daughter of the farmer who held or occupied the Queen's College Farm at Bramley Green. It was always called the College Farm. It is now called the Green Farm in consequence of its having first been sold to Mr. Thornton, of Beaurepaire, and then exchanged with the Duke of Wellington for other lands to make the two Estates more complete, with the Railway for the boundary.

William Cresswell farmed Bulls Down Farm. When he left Charles Butler, son of William Butler, senr., of Bramley Green, took it, and farmed it with his other little farm, Elliott's, belonging to W. W. B. Beach, Esq., of Oakley Hall, and this was exchanged in the second Duke's time for a farm called Cheesedown.

Jones' Farm took its name from its owner, an Irishman, who sold it to the Duke. Jesse Elliott, and then his son Daniel, were tenants. When Mr. Alington bought the reversion of the Brocas property he made an exchange with the Duke of Wellington— allotting part of this farm to Holly Cross Farm. Jones' Farm house has been very much improved by the present Mr. H. Welch Thornton. It was the first piece of building I think that he undertook since he became owner, and an excellent job he made of it, considering the tenant's comfort in every way. The bakehouse — one of the best I should say in the county—was built previously by the late Mr. A. Welch Thornton, his uncle. There is a good baking, grocery, bacon-curing, and corn merchant's business, as well as farming, carried on. The first shop was built by the Duke of Wellington in 1870.

Stocks Farm was occupied by the Clifts before 1700. After my grandfather, my uncle had it, but he left it owing to some dispute with Mrs. Brocas' agent. A Mr. Parsons then became tenant for a few years, and I came to the farm in 1864.

Under the chestnut tree on the Green used to be the parish whipping stocks. They were in a fair state of preservation when I first came here, but there is no vestige left now. The spot was a favourite playground for the children, and they, no doubt, helped to destroy them. On the Green the Bramley people held their Maying at Whitsuntide. This village festival is described by Miss Mary Russell Mitford in her book, "Our Village."

This was in the days when we went gipsying,
    A long time ago ;
When lads and lasses all in their best
    Were dressed from top to toe ;
They danced and sang their joking songs
    All on the forest green ;
Where nought but mirth and joviality
    All round us could be seen.

'Twas thus we passed those merry times :
    No thought of care or woe,
In the days when we went gipsying,
    A long time ago.
In the days when we went gipsying,
    - A long time ago.

The Upper Farm, so called, was at the time Miss Mitford visited Bramley, known as The Church Farm. It was occupied by my grandfather's eldest son and heir, Joseph, and two or three of my uncle's initials were cut in the brickwork of the front of the house. Mr. Thornton had them removed when he had the house renovated. There is some very fine old brickwork at the south end of the house, which Mr. Thornton left undisturbed. It is now called Middle Farm.

The Street Farm was occupied by the Holloways for many years. The old man was a blacksmith in Bramley Street, and his sons looked after the farm. There was a family of Haskers living in the parish for many years. I believe the last farm they occupied was the Street Farm.

To Park Gate Farm (Beaurepaire) Daniel Holloway came about the year 1835. He gave the farm up about 1850, and turned market salesman for different small farmers. This old Mr. Holloway used to tell the corn buyers to come to him to buy, as he could sell corn cheaper than the farmer, because they grew it and he did not. His daughter married the distinguished water-colour painter William Hunt, who painted many of his noted pictures of flowers and birds' nests in an upper room of the North Lodge. Hunt was the first to introduce moss backgrounds into his pictures, from specimens gathered in Bramley woods. Daniel Holloway's younger daughter died as recently as 1907.

When I was manager for Mrs. Brocas, Mr. Hunt would ask me sometimes to cut down a branch of a tree when he found the boughs darken his painting room. His pictures of village lads and noted characters were taken from the village folk, and the interiors of Bramley barns, with sacks of corn standing inside, and other buildings, furnished him with subjects. His portrait of Mesech Johnson, the weather-beaten follower of the hounds, is considered to be his finest work, and comparable with Rembrandt. I think, if my memory serves me right, Mr. Hunt painted old Mesech Johnson walking behind a cow, with an armful of green vetches held loosely under his arms. I remember the picture being much praised.

Reid's Farm was occupied by Mr. Reid. Next, by Charles Murrell, a land-drainer, who was largely employed by gentlemen round to undertake the drainage of their estates. After Murrell's death this farm was let, together with Latchmere Farm, to one of Elliott's sons, from Jones' Farm. Another farm at Latchmere was John Mulford's. After him came

William Matthews, brother to Thomas Matthews, of Lily Mill.

Of the noted characters of Bramley, much that is interesting might be told.

Mesech Johnson, whose portrait Hunt painted, was a constant follower of the hounds. He wore a scarlet-coat, cast off by some wealthier — but not keener—foxhunter than himself. He slept in barns and outhouses and lived "from hand to mouth." At last he was obliged to seek the refuge of the Union Workhouse, and after a short stay died there.

One, Thomas Allwright was very noted for his skill in curing the St. Vituses' dance—a malady we seldom hear of about here now. I have heard of doctors having cases of this ailment in hand which they could not cure, but the case being brought to Thomas Allwright the patient was cured.

Will Wheeler was our mole-catcher, and he made a good living in the winter months.

Barzillai Stroud was Mrs. Brocas' woodman. His father gave all his children Scriptural names. He was credited with telling fortunes by the stars and planets, and as a "wise man" was consulted when anything was lost or stolen. Once, when a garment was missing, he directed the owner to a certain house where a woman was washing clothes, and said she would find her missing property in the tub.

Joseph Fry was master of the Bramley Band, and also leader of the church music, the instrumental part of which was supplied by wind instruments. Our church choir was led by Joseph Fry and another playing clarionettes, and sometimes we had a German flute and two bassoons. There were two good bass singers, and one counteralto could sing clearly up to B flat. I could play, but was required to help the singing. Fry's services were in great request at all the "Mayings" and other festive occasions. He was a good musician, and kept the church music going at Bramley in the old style much longer than neighbouring villages did their's, but his band had to give place to an harmonium about 1860.

Old Stroud's musical ability was such that (so I have been told) he could stand in the porch of the Church while the choir was singing and set down all the parts correctly ; and he was a good copier of music. He was also a good penman ; and as a land-measurer he was employed to measure when the Commutation of Tithes was made. Before this it was customary for the farmers to go into the harvest fields and put a green bough on every tenth shock, called " Tithing the shocks." The parson did not always remove his shocks as quickly as he should, and this was a grievance to the farmer. Old Stroud was called " the cunning man. " He was supposed to tell people's destiny by planets, and if they had lost anything they would go to him for advice as to where to find it. I have been told that he first used to ask them where they were born, what day and what time of the day. He would then look up his books and tell them they were born under an unlucky planet or under a lucky planet as the case might be. There were people who believed in him.

Old Tom Leadbetter was famous for his dry sayings, which caused endless fun. I remember that Tom, on seeing a man who possessed a remarkably long nose, remarked "Wouldn't he do in the cherry country?" "Why?" he was asked. "Why, ye see, he could hang on the branches wi' his long nose, and pick the cherries wi' both hands."

Thomas Belcher lived at Hide House in the early forties—and I think much before that. He could not write, but could read, and had a thorough knowledge of the Scriptures, which he could repeat by the chapter.

George Stamp, a very good farm labourer, lived at Doll's Green, where the blacksmith's shop now stands, on the road to Sherfield. He was a married man, but had no family. George had an impediment in his speech, which sometimes caused amusement. His wife Eliza—"Our Hizer" was George's name for her—was for some reason or other, often running away from George. The house they lived in was of George's own building, or rather, construction. It was a mansion of clay and mud, the only bricks used being a few for the fireplace and chimney. It was roofed in and thatched with hoop chips, and was popularly called "Hoopchip Lodge, Doll's Green, Bramley, near Basingstoke." Yet for all the charms of the family mansion, "Our Hizer" would run away from George sometimes. Now, as George was a good manager, he made it a rule to fat a good hog to kill about Christmas, and " Our Hizer " invariably found her way home then, and kept herself very peaceable and quiet with George whilst the fat pig lasted. Then off she would go again, until tempted to return by the time the fat pig was ready again. On one occasion when she put in an appearance, after a long absence, to help George out with his fat pig, George's mother began to remonstrate with him for so meekly taking her in. "Well, our mudder," says George, "S'pose I was to wun away, and wun up all wound Wonnon, and wen I come back wouldn't you take me in again?" "Yes, be sure I I 'ood," says "Mudder." "Well," said George, triumphantly, "'Ats jest de same wi' our Hizer, ye know, mudder."

CHAPTER VI.

WHAT I REMEMBER ABOUT THE FARMS IN STRATFIELDSAYE.

When going to Mrs. Lavington's School at Stratfieldsaye, on entering that parish we came first to Perdue's Farm, occupied by John Fabery. He was often called "Macadam," from the fact that he planned and made the roads through the two parishes of Bramley and Stratfieldsaye. After Fabery, John Seward came to Perdue's Farm. He had been employed by the first Duke as a foreman bricklayer, and lived at the old Wyer's Farm in the corner of the Park near Chequer's Green. He had not been at Perdue long before the next farm, where one William Matthews lived, was laid to his farm. Matthews' house, which stood on the left side of the road leading to Mortimer, at Fair Oak Green, was pulled down, and a new house was built on the other side of the road, in Pound Close. The enlarged farm was called Perdue's, from the old farm, and is still so called.

There was also a small farm which stood in the corner of the field in Mill Lane and Folly Lane, with a barn, stable, and cottage. This farm was occupied by a man called Tailor Cane, who lived in the house afterwards owned by William Palmer.

Further along the Mortimer Road was a brickyard, worked by a Mr. Howard, who, I believe, came from Northampton. The kiln was done away with at last for want of suitable clay, the good clay being all used up. Mr. Howard lived in the large red-brick house on the hill on the left, where the house still stands.

I remember a great hue and cry being made—on a Saturday morning, I believe—that Long Pond was on fire. The people all ran to see the sight, but when they got there, they found it was the house, and not the pond that was on fire. Long Pond lay at the bottom of the hill, and Long Pond House in the field near to the pond.

Still further along the Mortimer Road we came to West End Green, where cricket matches were played, and other sports and pastimes carried on.

One Frank Thackham built himself a house here, and got a licence to sell beer. He called his house "The New House," and made a nice little fortune there. During the time the Reading and Basingstoke Railway was being made, he did a good trade with the navvies. Thackham was a man of exemplary character, and took care of his money when once he had got hold of it. I heard that from a young man he had always been saving ; and when, little by little, he had saved a sovereign, he tried to keep it safely by changing it into one gold piece, which he covered with cloth, and sewed on his coat for a button, thus always having it before him. But, though I heard this, I think, from what I knew of him, that he might be trusted to keep such a secret to himself. He had a family of three daughters and one son ; and I think I am right in saying that he gave them £500 or £600 each.

The Reading and Basingstoke Railway, just spoken of as a source of Thackham's prosperity, was intended to come through Stratfieldsaye. I can remember the "lights" cut through the hedges for it ; and I think I could now go and point out within a very few yards the course it was intended to take. It ran along the lower side of the farm, where Mr. Lunn now lives, near "Castleton," across his big field, over the road near Herriott's Farm (towards Fair Oak), past Southend Farm and Lily Mill to Sherfield Green. The original project was overthrown. It was said at the time that the first Duke of Wellington made objections to it being carried through his estate.

At Western Green, in the house now occupied by Mr. Holloway, the grocer, lived old Dr. Spence. He was, I believe, considered to be a very good doctor ; for, unlike Dr. Snipe, he never had a very long bill to pierce you with. He used to walk about carrying a big brown walking stick. He used to call at most of the public-houses—I suppose to enquire if they knew of anyone requiring his services. It was the custom then for people to be "blooded" in the arm : not much medicine was used in those days.

Near by, lived old Charley Holloway, the blacksmith, one of the best of men by nature. Charley used to make it a practice to be out in the road (if he saw anyone approaching) ready to have a word with most passers-by, who were not many in those days. If they were to his liking, he never got far with his talk with them before he would ask them if they would have a little drop of his gin ("ginney" he used to call it) ; and very soon "Mommie" (as he used to call his wife) was asked to bring the "ginney" out. "Mr. So-and-So is a-cold," or "come away without his great coat, and wants a little something to keep out the cold"— like old Dame Margery, Charley was good-natured in the extreme.

He had a way of making a chain-puzzle to fasten field gates, which the farmers often used : it consisted of a chain having a swivel slightly thinner one side than the other, so contrived that if anyone was not an adept hand, he could not undo it. I heard, when I went to school, of Lord Charles Wellesley trying once to open this puzzle-chain. Walking over the fields one day with his servant, he came to a gate fastened by one of them. His servant could not find out how to undo it ; and at last Lord Charles said to him "Get out of the way! I can undo old Charley Holloway's puzzles, I am sure!" and, I believe, he succeeded.

From Western Green, we go up a lane to Lavell's Farm, then held by Richard Ilsley, who also occupied Goulburn's and Dollery's Farms. He was considered a good farmer, and a quiet, good, all-round man. His family consisted of four sons, of whom three worked on the farm with their father, and the fourth was apprenticed to a tailor. The sons were unable to keep on the farm after their father's death.

Next following him was Robert Rogers, but he did not live long after he got there. His widow, with the assistance of a farm bailiff, kept on the farm, and managed it well. At her death her eldest son carried it on, but was at last obliged to give it up. Then it was taken on by Mr. Jacobs, whose son carries it on at the present time.

Next we come to Parsons' Farm. Mr. John Goddard farmed it, but not very successfully. After he gave it up, the Duke had it in hand for some time, when Mr. James Randall took it in 1850. This period was a very bad time for farmers—for a few years it was the most ruinous time for farmers I can remember.

Foreland's Farm was occupied by Luke Goddard. He took things rather easily, and was not a very successful farmer.

Chequers' Green Farm was held by the Monger family, but I do not think they did very well. The younger members of the family had to seek a living in other callings.

I remember going to this farm with David

Lavington, a schoolfellow of mine, on an errand. We were asked in ; and we found sitting beside the fire a very old-looking man. His appearance was such that we two boys sat and looked and looked at him, and did not know what to say ; we thought we should have burst out laughing. Presently the old man said, in a very gruff voice, "Where do you boys come from ?" That just gave us a chance to have something for an excuse to laugh at him ; for on our replying that we came from Bramley, he said "Oh, I am 94 years old, and have never been to Bramley !" Then we had freedom to laugh to the full.

King's Farm was held by William Rogers and his two brothers. He was a good farmer, and I think made the most of everything that came to his hand. His two brothers, John and David, took an active part in the work on the farm. They used to keep a good many cows, and fatted calves for veal. Old Mr. Keep, the butcher at Turgis, took nearly all the farmers' calves about here. He used to fetch them, take them home, kill, and weigh them. What he could not sell at home he used to put into hampers and send to the dead-meat market in London. Nothing was said about price when the calves were fetched from the farmers: that was not known until the quarter, or half-year's, account was made up. Then they had a meeting and settled up. Mr. Keep used to supply the farmers with most of the butcher's meat they had, and they always seemed to have great confidence in each other. It was the same with the gentlemen in the neighbourhood. If they wanted anything from a farmer, they would send an order for him to send them what they required, and never made it their point to ask, first, the price. This was the case for years when I first began business with the good old sort. But when the younger or more modern gentlemen took the place of such, they would, if dealing with the farmer, probably begin by asking the price, and then trying to get you to knock off something. So farmers had to learn a new lesson —to put on a little extra on that account, the knocking-off of which would make a deal. I remember once going to a gentleman who wanted some oats. I knew well enough, from previous deals I had had with him, that he would want something from the price I asked. So I put a couple of shillings on to have the fight with ; and in the end we made our deal at the price I intended to take. I went from him to another gentleman (I may remark they were both clergymen), and I asked him the same price I had at first asked the other. He at once said he would take them, and never once asked me to take anything off the price. I felt myself rather in a fix ; how was I to satisfy myself that I was doing them both justice ? I thought of a plan : and by winnowing his corn down extra well, I made them two or three pounds heavier per bushel ; and that, I thought, fairly met the case.

Ives' Farm, when I first remembered it, was tenanted by a Mr. Newcome. I believe he was a

Northamptonshire man ; he must have left somewhen early in the thirties. Following him was a Mr. John May, who was, I believe, a Welshman. I went to school with some of his family. One of his daughters afterwards settled in Reading ; she became proprietress of the Queen's Hotel, and died there not many years ago. John May's opinion about the Repeal of the Corn Laws was so strong that he made up his mind to give up farming if the Act came into force ; and he left the farm about the year 1848. That year he had an excellent bean crop ; and I believe he regretted leaving.

Then John and David Rogers took Ives' Farm. The Duke's agent, Mr. George Easton, was a good man to take land under, for he always seemed to give young beginners all the help he could to start them, if he saw they were people likely to prosper. The Duke's farms were always easier to get into than farms on other estates. The incoming tenant was always given the offer to work the fallows left him by the outgoing tenant, which was a great help to them ; and the Lady Day rents were not asked for until November, so that the new tenant had one harvest before he was asked to pay any rent. This mode of letting in gave a young beginner, with small capital, great facilities on getting into a farm.

Adjoining Ives' Farm is Southend Farm. My uncle Jesse left Stocks Farm in 1835 and took Southend Farm, in succession to one John Lavington. Southend Farm was then very much out of condition

and the buildings dilapidated. Previously there used
to be a little farm at the back of the old "Fighting
Cocks" at Fair Oak, where Daniel Holloway used to
live. When he left this little farm it was laid to
Southend, and afterwards the farm formerly held by
Charles Tubb, who once lived at Hayward's Farm,
was also added. So that these farms added together
formed the new Southend Farm—altogether between
three and four hundred acres—which my uncle took,
He, being an excellent farmer, in time brought it all
round into good condition, and when he had it in
order he grew the finest crops I ever saw. The
people working on the farm used to say that there
was not a bushel of couch to be found all over the
farm. It was a great thing to say, but I think it was
not far from correct. My uncle's family consisted
of one daughter only. I occasionally went to spend
an evening with them. My cousin Jane was musical,
and as I was too, we had pleasant evenings together.
My uncle was noted for his sleeping powers. In
the evening he would sit beside the fire, with his
back against the wall, sleeping soundly, until roused
by my aunt with "Come, Jesse, wake up!" I
remember being told that he went fourteen years
courting my Aunt (Miss Charlotte Moss) before he
married her, and that he slept half of the time when
courting her! He must have thought courting and
sleeping combined very enjoyable. One night when
I had been to see them at Southend, and was
returning home, I saw something lying in the road.

Having been told that a ghost had been seen somewhere in that road (Mill Lane) I began to think I was approaching it, so I went up close to it and gave it a good kick. It gave a groan, and after a while I found it was Charles Lavington, who, I suppose, had been spending the evening at the "Fighting Cocks," and was taking a short rest before finishing his journey home. I heard of another man going down Mill Lane, in the middle of the night, and just about at the same spot. He saw something which he could not quite make out, and fearing to go up to it, he began walking backwards to get away from it. To his terror, what he thought was the ghost followed him. He kept going backwards until he got home. Still facing the supposed ghost he drew himself backwards through the door, into the house, and having carefully fastened doors and windows, went to bed. Next morning, when he opened his door, he found lying outside a young donkey, which had not long been foaled. That was the supposed ghost! The man happened to go down the lane before the foal was strong enough to recognise its mother, so it came staggering along after him instead of staying with its mother. I never heard of any ghost in Mill Lane after that.

Going back to say something more about my uncle's farming, I think I may fairly say that the whole parish was improved in farming by his example, and all seemed to speak of him as their leader. I

remember being shown a letter written by the Great
Duke to my uncle on some matters connected with
the farm.   And I also remember that the writing was
very difficult to read.   I thought he could not have
gone to old Daniel Sweetzer's school the same as I
did, or it would have been written much plainer.   My
uncle's high state of management and cultivation was
much admired and spoken of, far and near.   And I
have been told by a person who used to visit my uncle
at that time that the Great Duke spoke of his tenant
at Stratfieldsaye as being such an ideal farmer that
one of the noblemen sent his steward from afar to
look over my uncle's farm.   My uncle gave up
up the farm entirely through my aunt (his second
wife).   She was always telling him, and at last
persuaded him that he was too old to look after it
and keep it in first-class condition.   Mr. John Butler,
of Sherfield Court Farm, on hearing that my uncle
intended giving up Southend, offered him £500 for
the goodwill if he would let him have it for one
of his sons, and he told me that he would have
given more rather than have lost it.   A Mr. Boxall,
who, I think, was a friend of my aunt's, got it
out of my uncle by allowing him £80 a year as
long as he lived, and he only lived two years
afterwards.   I may say here that when a young
man my uncle never did the practical work on the
farm for my grandfather as my father did.   My
father at the age of about fifteen took charge of the
second team as carter, and he was, as I know well,

an excellent ploughman. Good ploughing was much studied in those days — and the land required it, and so it does now—and the talk among carters was generally of their teams — which was the best, and best looked after, and who was the best ploughman. Ploughing matches were also kept up in the summer, and the carters were keen in contesting for the prizes. The first prize was something useful to the carter who won it—perhaps a new hat. The lowest prize was a "Whizzel shooter"—a round, rough felt hat with the brim turned up all round, for the wearer to see better with next time he competed for a prize. The winner of this became a laughing-stock for the other men. When I began working at home as a boy, I used often to be working with Tom Leadbetter. He told me that when he was a boy he used to ride about the fields in an old gig with my grandfather to open the gates and wait upon him. One of the tales he told was about my grandfather and uncle. My grandfather told my uncle Jesse one day that he wanted him to go to plough, for he thought he was quite big enough. But uncle, who did not quite see it in the same light, replied "Well, father, a cow is big enough to catch a hare—if she could run fast enough, you know."

Lily Mill was held by Thomas Matthews. The old house then stood just over the back stream near to the old mill, and was reached by going down a watery lane. It was pulled down by Mr. George

Easton, the then steward, and a new house was built upon higher ground, where it still stands, and is a very great improvement on the old house. A new road was made by it to the mill, and also on towards Sherfield. Mr. Matthews was a very quiet and good company sort of man, and a counter-alto singer in Bramley Church, where I have sung with him many a time. He used to take the solo parts in our anthems ; and one of the songs which he used to sing when we had a festive gathering (our rent dinners) ran something like this :—

In all your transactions let this be your plan :
Seek welfare for others as well as you can ;
Do your duty, love mercy, unite all together
And travel through life like birds of a feather.

If you meet with a pilgrim whose way has been lost,
And through life's rugged paths has been troubled
    and crossed,
Take him home to your cottage to nourish his blood,
And cheer up his spirits with something that's good.
    So in all your transactions, etc.

If you meet with a female who has gone astray,
Or been by some artful villian deluded away,
Pity her weakness, and soften her pain,
And persuade her from going the same road again.
    So in all your transactions, etc.

Mr. Thos. Matthews had two sons and one daughter. His elder son Henry became a miller, and his son now occupies the mill at Sherborne St. John which his father (Henry) occupied and in which he died.

Thomas, the younger son, went on with Lily Mill Farm, but he did not occupy it for many years. After him it was taken by Mr. Butler, son of Mr. James Butler, of Perdue's Farm, who still occupies it.

I have seen many improvements made in Stratfieldsaye in my remembrance. Several farmhouses were newly-built, with good homesteads added, and put on fresh ground. Mr. George Easton, I always thought, displayed good judgment in this as well as in the many other new roads he made.

James Hall, the first Duke's keeper, lived where Mr. Dodd, the tailor, now lives ; and the five double houses on that side were built when I went to school, as was also the Infant School. I helped to nail up some of the palings, in my dinner hours, when the school was built. Some time after that the old Bull Lane was done away with, and replaced by that very capital road which we find there now. The road from Broadford Bridge to the Wellington Arms was cut straight and made good. The new road that was cut through part of the Pheasantry was made by Mr. Abel Easton, and the old road which went through the Park and came out at Chequer's Green was then done away with.

While speaking of Stratfieldsaye as it was in the Great Duke's time, I may mention that I attended his funeral at St. Paul's in 1852. The tenants were all invited to his funeral, and all had tickets for seats in St. Paul's. I remember going to see him lying in state at Chelsea Hospital. I saw the funeral, but not as a ticket-holder. The funeral car, drawn by twelve black horses was an impressive sight ; and so, indeed, was the whole procession. So great was the crowd expected to be that all traffic was stopped at an early hour the previous evening ; and the road the funeral had to pass over was sprinkled with gravel : it was so, I remember, where I saw the funeral pass.

The autumn of 1852 was an extremely wet one, and the floods were very high. The railway engines running between Reading and Paddington had their fires put out, the floods being so high.

I believe the tenant farmers were well considered that year on the Duke's Estate, through the assistance of his excellent Steward, Mr. George Easton, and I know of many other instances of this kind of thing being done, when there was real necessity for it ; and it was done in a noble and satisfactory way. I have known that when those who on the Estate cultivated a bean crop (as was very largely done in the past) had a blight take them, as happened occasionally, they found, on the rent day, that it had all been considered by landlord and steward both ; and something was handed back to help to meet the loss sustained.

When I first took to going to the audits, the evenings passed with song and glee. I should like to give the words of the chorus of a song sung by old Mr. Thomas Matthews, which were these :—

> " Brave Wellington with Blucher joined,
> Which made proud Boney yield,
> After a long, fierce, raging fight,
> To fly the crimson field,
> To fly the crimson field."

I went to the dinner given in celebration of the erection of the Great Duke's monument at the London Lodge on Heckfield Heath. All the tenants, both from the Stratfieldsaye and Wolverton Estates, sat down together in the Tennis Court at the Duke's house. I forget the total number ; but I believe they were all subscribers to the monument. I also went to see Queen Victoria when she came to visit the Duke about the year 1845.

In the first Duke's time, before the railway was made, as the Judges passed through on their Western Circuit to Winchester for the Assizes, they used to call at Stratfieldsaye House and dine with the Duke. It caused great excitement in the neighbourhood, and people for miles round would go and see the tables laid for dinner. I believe the blinds of the windows were left up for the people to see the company when they were all seated. The High Sheriff, with his javelin-men, escorted the Judge to Winchester. Since Sir Robert Peel brought in his police (Peelers they were called) the office of escort has been filled by them.

CHAPTER VII.

FARMING IN THE OLD DAYS.

I consider that the farmers used to take much greater pains with their farming than they do now; and the land required it. There were no underground drains, and but little of the land was chalked. Fields were very small, with wide hedges, and the ploughs needed three or four horses to draw them, all walking singly in the furrow. All work then was done by hand. No labour-saving machines existed; manual labour was necessary in every process of farming. Ploughing, sowing, reaping, mowing—manual labour did all. I have already spoken of the seedsman with his seedlip, which is now supplanted by the drill. A capable seedsman could sow very evenly, all over alike, the whole field. If his master sent him into a 10-acre field with 20 bushels of corn, when it came up you could see no difference. This was very keenly looked after by the master. Beans had to be set, one by one, by hand. In mowing and reaping hard manual labour was required for the use of scythe and hook; and all thrashing was done by the flail. This instrument consisted of two sticks tied together. The handle was made of ash, with a ferule at the smaller end, having what we called a "start" fixed in it, with a head to it, which held the "cappance."

This "cappance" was made of a piece of ash grooved out to fit the "start." It was bound to the "start" by a piece of waxed thread, but fixed so as to work round freely on the "start." The other stick, which was called the "swingell," was the part which beat out the corn, and was a knotty crab-stick, which being very hard, was found the best for the purpose. This swingell had also a leather cappance tied on firmly, and the two sticks, the handstaff and swingell were tied together by a piece of white leather thong, cut for the purpose. We, who knew how to use them, knew well how to put them together. I have myself been thrashing with flail many a day in winter time when there was not much other work to do. My father used to keep two men at work, thrashing wheat for eight or nine months in the year, say from Michaelmas (or a little before) to May. A flail is now but rarely to be seen. A rhyme about thrashing, often quoted in my young days, ran thus :—

> The men with crabsticks thrashed the corn,
> They whipped it skin from bones ;
> The miller served it worse than that,
> He ground it 'tween two stones.

The farmers then took great pains to make their men good husbandmen. My uncle Jesse used great patience and perseverance in his business as farmer, particularly in the training of the young labourers. He was a great employer of labour, particularly of women and boys. Everyone had a job if they went to him for one. The boys' first job was

most often to go with two horses to harrow, and a
a boy new to the work would receive particular
attention from my uncle.   I recall to mind his
following a boy at work, calling out such directions
as " Keep Jack up, boy!"   " Steady, Poppet!"
"Keep the harrow over-right, boy!"   "Casn't thee
see, boy? If not, look behind!"   And when turning
at the end to come back, he would say "Now boy,
keep 'em both up to the hedge, and turn on the
headland and don't tread the ends of the lands."
The boy who followed his advice was speedily taught
to make himself a good husbandman.   I have no
doubt though, that the boy was glad when it was
time for uncle to go to dinner, though it was pretty
certain that he would be back before it was the
boy's time to go home.   Following the harrows, there
was almost always a little tribe of women with their
"lap-bags" on, to pick up every weed or root they
could see on the surface, which should not be there,
and carry them to the hedge and throw them away.
And he always had a man or two when ploughing
for seed in the field, to keep the furrows open with
spade and pick, in case heavy rain came on, which
he liked to see run off as fast as it fell.   My uncle
Jesse, in his farming, combined patience with perseverance, and his efforts were crowned by large crops
resulting.   He was quite the model farmer of that
day.   He believed in giving the land every attention
possible.   And not land only, but every head of live
stock on the farm was well cared for and kept in

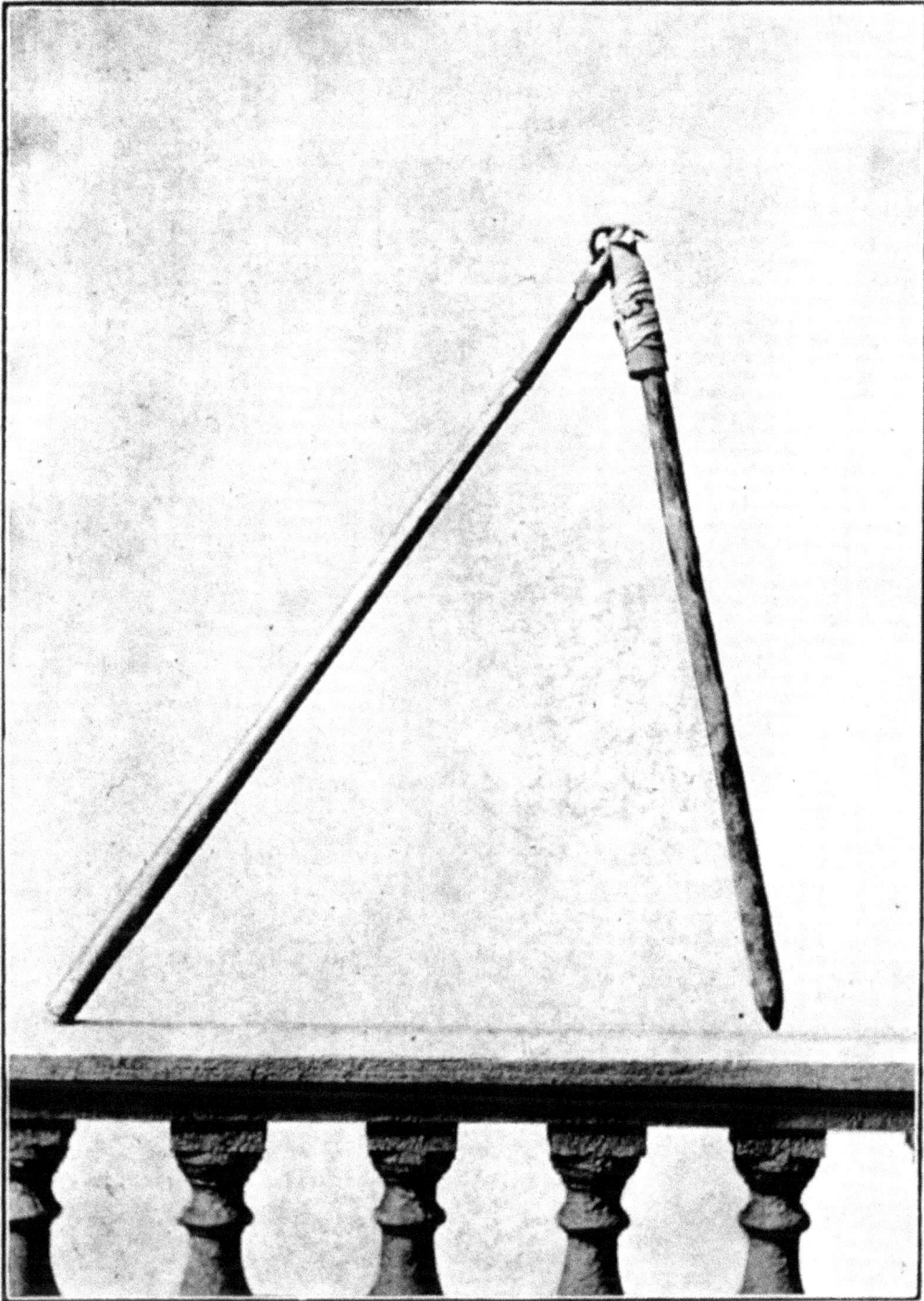

The Old Flail.

the best of condition. When uncle left this farm to go to Stratfieldsaye, his old labourers followed him. We used to see old James Chandler and John Neville going plodding along, each helped by two sticks to their work at Stratfieldsaye. This they continued to do as long as they were able, passing Hollow Cross each morning about five o'clock.

I have said a good deal about my uncle Jesse's good farming, and I must now say a little about my father, and what he did at farming. He was not able to spend so much money on small matters in his farming, and therefore his farm was not kept in such neat and apple-pie order as my uncle's. He had his ten children to rear and bring up, which he did on a farm of about 190 acres. In this way he, as I consider, proved himself the better man of the two. My father was a working farmer, strong and active, and able to do any sort of work on the farm, and he was the best ploughman and seedsman that I ever saw take a seedlip in his hand. My uncle could do none of these things, but my father put us all to the work as we got old enough. I have been in the barn thrashing with the flail many a day. We, the boys, six in number, were brought up to use any sort of tool there was on the farm. So I think he well deserved the name of a good father, and quite equal to the times he lived in.

Bean setting was a great business. It began about February 14th. Women and boys used to meet

at the granary door about 8 a.m. or soon after for
their daily allowance of seed beans, which was four
gallons for a woman, two gallons for a big strong boy
or girl, and a gallon for a smaller child. The price
paid was 3d. or 4d. per gallon: so that supposing a
woman had two children to help her she might add
12s. or 13s. to her husband's earnings in a week.
Good and quick setters could earn more. The time
they were in the field was from 8.30 to 2.30 ; seldom
later. The beans were planted thus: A "setting-
stick" was used to make the holes. "One hole, one
bean," was the rule, and good, practised hands could
move very quickly, with the setting-stick in one hand,
and the other hand full of beans, following, dropping
one bean only in each hole as fast as the holes could
be made. When the beans came up, the work was
generally overlooked to see if there had been anyone
playing foul, and dropping more than one bean in
one hole, which was the case sometimes. Bad setters,
who could not keep pace with others, would put a
handful in a hole, now and then, to get rid of them.
When this was proved by the growth of the beans,
we used to get some of the setters together, and on
the spot itself try and discover the defaulters ; and
generally we could find them out.

Bean planting used to take about a month.
When we had about half done, we used to have what
we called a "middlings." This meant an extra little
bit of lunch on that day, and an extra half-pint of
beer. This special lunch was often partaken of in

empty pondholes in which we could find shelter from the cold winds, enjoy our lunch, and make ourselves as jovial as possible by passing jokes with one another. Then, at the end of the planting time, we had a "finishing-up-day" to look forward to, when there was a hot dinner cooked, and plum puddings made. We used to have an old goose who produced a double-yoked egg or two each year; and these eggs were always used for the "bean-feast puddings." When dinner was over, and the women had sat a little while by a big roasting fire in the kitchen, father paid them their wages. There were in all from twelve to twenty of them. We boys, while the paying was taking place, used to be free to play outside, often at marbles. The women always seemed well pleased with what they had earned.

Women, when at bean-setting, used to come to work in a brown round smock, such as their husbands used to wear. They had loops on the inner side of their petticoats at the bottom, and strings on the outer sides in front; and these were tied before they began work. "Tying the breeches" this was called; and various ribald jokes and rhymes were current at bean-setting time.

For two or three years, when I first began work, I used to go a bean-setting with the other setters; for father did not forget to put us all to such work as we were most capable of doing, when once we started work.

Bean-setting over, the next work women were called to do was the hoeing of wheat, which began as soon as the plant was strong enough ; this was begun about the middle of April, and carried on until haymaking. And, in my opinion, this wheat hoeing is not nearly enough practiced in these days.

Haymaking was most methodical ; and great pains were taken. After the mowers came the " tedders," tedding out the grass with prongs. Next we had to "wind-rake" it : that is draw it together with rakes into small rows, and then next day into beds, and turn it over once in the day. At night it was put into "half-cocks." Next day it was thrown out again, turned over, and finally got up into "full cock." It was then nearly ready to carry. Each woman had to find a rake and prong of her own. We had no sort of machinery to assist in those days.

Harvest came soon after the haymaking ; and this gave a full month's work, or more, to the women and children. Some families used to ask their employers to let them go out to where corn ripened sooner than here (say at Chichester, or some such forward place) ; there they could get a fortnight's harvest work before our corn was ready. And after harvesting our corn, they would ask for another fortnight to go into more backward counties (say, Wiltshire or elsewhere) and get another two or three weeks' work.

After harvest came the hop-picking, when a man with a large family could earn several pounds. Hops were grown in Bramley in my early days, and rather largely at one time ; and there were several hop-kilns in the parish, which were turned into cottages when hop-growing ceased to be practised. There is something rather peculiar about the growth of hops. They are in some way similar to the French bean (or scarlet runners, as some call them). Their leaves are somewhat similar, and they both grow up poles. As soon as the bine (as we call it) gets a few inches long, the poles are put to them, and in a day or two, or in a very short time after, if you go to them you will find their leading spire, or bine, drawing itself up to the pole, but a hop will take its course round the pole with the sun, viz., from east, south to west. A French bean will take the opposite course and go from east, north, west, to south, against the sun. There is no way of preventing this that I know of, and no accounting for it. The hop will run quicker up a maplewood pole than any other. This is accounted for because maplewood is warmer than any other wood.

It has been said in my hearing how bad the times were in the old days. But I do not consider that they were bad, for as I have shown in this chapter, all work was done by manual labour ; and not only the man received wages, but his wife and children had opportunities to earn a good many pounds to add to his wages. Besides regular farm-work, the "acorning" season brought the family a good sum. I have known families to pick up one hundred bushels, and some much more, of acorns, and sell them at 1s. per bushel. I have made these remarks about the earnings of the labouring class to show that they could earn good money in my early days, when they were free to take up the work they chose : and when I have heard of the "bad times" of the past days, I have felt inclined to refute it, knowing that what I have here written is true, and from my own experience. Since I wrote this I have narrowly looked over what women and children would reasonably earn during the year at out-of-door work, to be added to the men's wages, They could, and did, look after their cottages as well, then as now. My calculation proves to me that it amounted to from fifteen to eighteen pounds a year, or say from six to seven shillings per week for the year round. I have taken this statement to a good old woman who is still living, at the age of nearly ninety years, who has, with her husband, worked for me for nearly half of that time. She verifies it to be correct.

There were always labourers who saved money, and, of course, others who did not. An old man named Abraham Wheeler worked for my father when I was a boy, and it was said many times in my hearing that he in his early days saved eighty pounds. Unfortunately for him, he lent it to a farmer named Adam Tubb, living at Adam Tubb's Farm (so called)

at the lower end of this parish, and he lost it all.
An old man whom we called "Carpenter Woods"
left five or six hundred pounds, I was told, when
he died. Some others of the labouring class owned
small portions of land, as can be proved by an old
map of Stock's Farm in my possession. Several
pieces round the outskirts of the farm were owned by
others, my ancestors among the rest. The Clifts
owned from thirty to forty acres besides Hollow Cross,
but from want of building accommodation on such
small lots, they were compelled to sell to those who
owned the adjacent larger farms, which had good
buildings to them.

CHAPTER VIII.

WORK INSIDE THE FARMHOUSE.

While the men were busy outside at work, no less busy were the womenfolk inside. Beside all the household work required to be done in a modern house, all baking and brewing had to be done at home, and the women were kept continually at work. It was work, so called, but I think many of them took a great pleasure in it. The time went harder with many of them if they could not do it. The labourers, as well as the farmers, baked their own bread. Our charwoman, Betty Bennett, could bake as good a loaf as anyone, and we often used to have a loaf of her baking brought to us for a change. The loaves we made were very large, and were often too bitter, being made with home-made yeast. To remedy the bitterness, they used to put into the leaven nobs or pieces of charcoal from wood embers. A few potatoes were also used in the bread-making. One day in the week was allotted out for the baking, and the bread was made to keep a week. The labourers used to get in from the mill half a sack of flour at a time: baking at home made it go much further.

Once a month we brewed. For brewing we used to grow our own barley, and have so much made into malt—enough for the year. The malt when brought home was put into a dry bin in the granary, to keep the atmosphere from slacking it, until wanted for use. Hops were grown in the parish. The process of brewing was this : A copper of water was boiled the last thing before going to bed, the mash-tub being set on a stand close to the copper, with the "huck-muck" and stirrer ready for use. We went to bed a little earlier than common, so that we could get up at four o'clock next morning, make the copper boil up afresh, and empty it into the mash tub. We let it stand till the steam was off enough to see one's face clearly reflected in the water, when it was considered to be at the right temperature for "mashing" —putting in the malt. (We did not know anything about thermometers for taking the right tempera-tures.) The copper was refilled with water, and made to boil again. The mash tub was then filled up, and let stand for so long ; then the "sweetwort" was let run into an under tub. After the mash tub had again been filled from the copper, the sweetwort from the under tub was placed in the copper with the hops, and boiled, simmering for about half an hour. Then it was taken out of doors and strained through a hop sieve into cooling tubs. When we considered it cool enough, we brought it in again, and put it into deeper tubs, and there let it stand until it got about the warmth of cows' milk or a little below. Then the yeast was added, and a handful of flour was sprinkled over it and well worked about with the "piggen"—a bowl made of a particular shape for its own purpose in brewing. The wort was left in the tubs for two nights and one day. On each morning the yeast was skimmed off. Then it was put into barrels, and was called beer. We left the vent open for about a week, keeping the barrels well filled up, and skimmed off the yeast as often as required. When judged fit, it was then bunged down.

In using three and a half bushels of malt we made a half-hogshead of "ale," with a few gallons over; and a half-hogshead of "small beer" and a few buckets over. The two lots left over were "married"—that is, put together in a small barrel for a "go-first" as we used to call it, and used while the larger barrels were getting into better condition. The ale was used in the house, and the small beer in the fields, at lunch time, and so on. We used to carry it in wooden bottles. Beer drinks sweeter out of wooden bottles than anything.

Strong beer was made twice a year, when an extra two, or it may be more, bushels of malt were put into the mash to make a half-hogshead of strong beer, which was generally left untouched for six months, by which time it would be thoroughly clear. When tapped, it was not brought out to everybody, but mostly kept for father and his friends to enjoy while smoking their long pipes in the evening. It was served in long (or deep) glasses, small at the bottom, and bell topped. Such glasses we do not see now-a-days. Good beer always looked well in these glasses. (I have heard sometimes of the key of the barrel being lost). I never was such a clever brewer as a man I once heard of, who could brew eight sorts of beer from one peck of malt, each kind being appropriately named thus:— (1st) "Touch-crown," (2nd) "Merry-go-down," (3rd) "Table beer," (4th) "Trim," (5th) "Swish-swash," (6th) "Dish-dash," (7th) "........ache," and (8th) "Thin."

Washing days were pleasant enough, generally, but not on wet days. But wet or fine, Betty Bennett always found a way to get over it pretty peacefully and quietly. Everything was done by rule. On Friday the "lye" was run. This lye was the water prepared for the washing of clothes. It was made by passing clean water through clean wood ashes. A wooden frame about eighteen inches square was used, in which a layer of clean wheat straw was placed, at the bottom ; and on this a coarse cloth of large size was laid, and filled full of the ashes. Then water was poured on it, as much as it would hold, and the water would drip slowly through into a large vat or tub. It was a long job, and took from the Friday to the Monday afternoon. It was a month's washing for ten of us. The actual washing was commenced at three o'clock on Monday morning, when Betty Bennett would come and call up my sister. My eldest sister would get up and let her in, and help her to do the washing-up till daylight (or, say, seven o'clock), when the second woman would arrive to help with the washing, leaving my sister free to attend to us, and do the housework. The washing itself was finished about mid-day on Tuesday. Then father would make up a good ironing fire, so that the day might be made out in ironing. On Wednesday, Betty came again to continue the ironing, with my sister's help, and by Thursday all articles would be finished and put away, clean, into the tub-house, so called. "A place for everything, and everything in its place" was a maxim my father always strictly enforced.

CHAPTER IX.

EXPERIENCES AT GRAZELEY.

I have been writing recollections of my earlier days, and am now going to write up the events as they came to me in my after life. In 1848 I left home and went to live at Grazeley, near Reading, with Mr. Daniel Davis. He was a large farmer there, and farmed the whole of the parish. There were three farm homesteads in it. The farm I lived at was called Fuller's Farm. Mr. Davis' mother and youngest sister, Esther, kept the house, and I lived with them. Mr. Daniel and his sister Deborah lived at the lower farm. One of their sisters, who married a Mr. Stevens, lived at another farm called Mearands. One of Mr. Stevens' sons had been living with his grandmother Davis and Aunt Esther, helping his uncle Daniel to look after the farm. He left his uncle to take a corn merchant's business in Reading. I was told about the vacancy, and went and saw Mr. Davis and got the situation. The Davises and Clifts had been associated for years before, but I had never seen them until I went to live with them. Their elder brother Thomas married my father's elder sister, Ann Clift, and started in business here at Barefoot's Farm, which we have in our occupation still. I have referred to him previously as having killed nine partridges out of ten at one shot. His gun was his downfall in business. Anything of this sort was very unlike the Clift family.

On taking up my situation with Mr. Daniel Davis, I was to have one pound a month, with all found. I never thought much about money matters. I had only been taking it in very small lots ; but "never despise the day of small things," or, as the Scotsmen say, "Many mickles make a muckle." I put what I had saved at home, which was twenty-five pounds, into the London and County Bank in Reading at interest, and made do on the money I was taking. I very soon got settled down with Miss Hester and her mother. I received great kindness from them all during the six years I was with them. Being the only man residing in the house I had the lion's share of attention, and have always looked back with much satisfaction upon sharing their home comforts and the society of a higher class than I had been used to before. This will be easily understood when it is remembered that I lost my mother when I was eight years old, and as one of a family of ten was brought up by my sisters and father. I entered on my service with Mr. Davis on October 10th, 1848. The Reading and Basingstoke Branch of Railway had not started running then. The first passenger train was run through Grazeley from Basingstoke to Reading on November 4th, 1848. The work I was first put to do in my new situation was to look after the sheep and fill up my spare time in anything I saw wanted doing. At times I was left a good deal to myself. Mr. Davis was fond of sport— shooting and coursing. He occupied the whole of Grazeley, about five hundred acres, a tithing or liberty of Sulhampstead Banaster or Sulhampstead Mailes, I am not certain which. There was no church at Grazeley, but the family had a sitting in one of the Sulhampstead Churches, though they mostly used to go into Reading to St. Mary's Episcopalian Chapel in Castle Street. In the evening they attended a little chapel near home, called Pound Green Chapel. Miss Deborah was organist there; she began her music rather late in life, and therefore could not play very well. I had been in the Church Choir at home, and could play the flute fairly well, and I was soon asked to join her choir. I could play a little on several different instruments, but had never had a chance of trying to play an organ or a piano. However, I had not been there more than about a month when, one evening, I thought I would go down to the Chapel and see what I could do on the organ. I took my flute, went and got the key of the chapel, took some lights, and went and locked myself in and began to try what I could do on the organ. It had a foot pedal to it so that I did not want anyone to blow for me. I then made B flat on the flute, and worked my fingers up the keyboard of the organ and found the same note. When I had got these two notes to be the same on both instruments I knew what would follow by

ascending or descending. Having got the scales right
in this way, I began to pick out tunes with my
right hand, looking first to notes then to fingers.
Then I had to get my left hand to work with the bass.
This I found a great difficulty, but, however, the
evenings being long, I used to take every opportunity
I could to have a couple of hours or so at the
organ. The first time I was able to play with both
hands at once, that is treble and bass, I was so
delighted with the advancement that I hardly knew
how to leave the organ to go home. I kept strictly
to practice, going and locking myself in (to prevent
anyone else doing so), thus practising quite by myself, and having no teaching by anyone. In six
weeks from the time I began practising, Miss Deborah
asked me to play to the congregation during service,
which I did. I was able to say then that I could
play on six instruments and never had a lesson.

A year or two after this there was a new district
Church, built just outside of Grazeley, in Shinfield
parish. It was called Grazeley District Church.
When it was consecrated and opened, we attended, and
I joined the choir. The gentleman who put in the
organ, Mr. Merry, undertook the playing of it, but
soon got tired of the job. The Rev. Theophilus
Saulez, the minister, asked me to undertake it, which
I did, and at the same time led the singing. I always
felt I could play best when I could keep the singing
going—it sort of hid the mistakes when I made any
in the playing. So on a Sunday I had my sheep to

look after, and do what was required to them for the day, and be up early, sometimes quite by five o'clock in the morning, to get it done in order to go to Church in time for service. Then I went to see the sheep again as soon as I came out of Church, before I had my dinner. In the afternoon I used to go to them again and do what was necessary, then off to Church for the afternoon service. After that was over I went back to the sheep to do what was required for the night, then home to tea and be ready to go to Pound Green Chapel at six o'clock to play their organ.

Mr. Daniel Davis and Miss Deborah always came to dine with Miss Esther at our house on Sundays. They never failed to do this, on account of their mother being there, and after she died they always kept up the same rule.

Old Mrs. Davis died here on April 19th, 1849. There was a deep snow on the ground at that time, and she was buried while the snow was still about. I was asked to attend the funeral with the family. Her age was 96 years. The family all lived to a great age.

The vicinity of Grazeley was rather notable for its celibacy. I think if one took a circle of about two miles from Fuller's Farm, where I was living, you could find nearly twenty bachelors, and almost I may say, as many spinsters. Among the spinster ladies I must not forget to name Miss Mary Russell Mitford, who I used often to see out in the dusk

of the evening. She was seldom seen out by daylight,
and she walked with her maid following a short
distance behind her. I occasionally found them
taking shelter from the storm in our carthouse, which
stood beside the road. I never saw her with an
umbrella that I remember. I believe she had an
objection to them, and had been known to say that
a good wetting through to the skin did people good.
I have been told that she was very peculiar in home
life. She was very fond of her dog—May, I think it
was called, and I believe she had one or two other
dogs beside, all of which lived pretty much in her
bedroom, as I was told. Miss Mary Russell Mitford
was, I believe, connected with the Russell family
living at Swallowfield Park. She died in 1855 and
was buried at Swallowfield. I used to think Grazeley
was very much brightened up by the talent of the
people living in the neighbourhood. Miss Mitford
stood first with her book "Our Village," in
which she brings in Bramley parish, and speaks
of the "Mayings" being held there near the stocks
— that is the whipping stocks which stood under
the chestnut tree just in front of my house
where I am writing this. Another lady poet was
found in Miss Mary Kent, whose pen mostly
touched upon the gay young gallants, and spoke of
her going to the little sanctuary, as she called it,
where, if she went, she was certain to see a pair of
pretty eyes peeping through the curtain. Certainly,
Miss Deborah's organ pew was large enough to take
in her choir, and had a rail and curtain round it.

Old Mr. Daniel Davis was a very intelligent and well informed man. He must, I think, have read himself up a good deal in his earlier days. He was a great speaker (and snuff taker), fond of sport, kept three or four greyhounds, and shot. I had put into my hands for my use when I first went there a double-barrel flint gun. I could not do much with that. I had been used to a little percussion-cap gun at home before I went there. I remember one of my exploits in wild duck shooting when I was at Grazeley. I was one morning walking round the farm, and when about half a mile away from home I saw five wild ducks go over and settle in a pond in a quiet, remote part of the farm further on. So I went back home, got my musket, and went to the spot to see if I could get at them. There was a high hedge running down not far off from the pond, but the sun was shining brightly at the time, and I was afraid they would see my shadow through the hedge. So I watched my opportunity, and when I saw them all diving their heads under water at the same time I seized my chance of moving forward until I got near enough to fire. Coming up to them they all had their heads under water and their tails upwards. I at once took my opportunity and fired, and knocked most of them over on their backs. I ran down to the pond thinking I was going to have three or four of them to take home, but up they got and away they flew as if nothing had happened. I don't think they did know what had happened, for as their tails were upwards and their heads under water they did not hear the report of the gun. So my advice is when you go to shoot wild ducks — 'never fail to shoot at their heads, and not at their tails.

The Misses Davis (both Miss Deborah and Miss Esther) were well read and intelligent. Miss Esther would ask me in winter evenings to read to her, which was quite a new thing for me to do. The first book she gave me to read was " Cook's Voyages round the World," and I got quite to like it. I took "Chambers' Journals," which I considered very edifying. I also took the " Exeter Hall Lectures to Young Men," which were given through the winter months every year. These, and several other good useful books, were got for me by a gentleman who used to come and preach at the Pound Green Chapel.

There was another family living near—the Smith family (three sons and one daughter). One son used to write a good deal. I had another good family of associates — the Horsburgh family, living at Wokefield Park Farm (three sons and two daughters)—a very intelligent family, seeming to make merriment in every way; they were Scotch people. There was always an open door and a welcome as often as I could go there. They were well up to all sorts of games and jollifications. The old people seemed to be as good as people could be. One of the sons took me to Scotland for a month's holiday with him. It was a month of real enjoyment, too. The father and the same son and myself went there together once after that. I thought it a good country for a young farmer to pay a visit to.

I left Grazeley in October, 1854, after completing six years' service without a rise in pay. But I look back upon it as six years of well spent time for me in my early life : not altogether in farming, for I considered my father was a far better tiller of the soil and a better farmer than Mr. Davis was, but the knowledge I got in farming at home before I went there, and the pushing up I got there added to it, fitted me for a better position to get elsewhere than if I never had gone there. I was not out of a situation very long before I heard of another at Bradfield, in Berks. It was to take the entire management of a farm for a widow— Mrs. Chillingworth. I went to see her and got it. This proved a great step up for me. I had £15 per quarter, the best bed in the house, and a good table provided for me. She had a family of six children, mostly all at school. She gave me full power to manage, and supported and encouraged me to do my best, which I must say I did, to the best of my knowledge ; and she really seemed to look upon me as if I was one of the white hen's chickens and could never do wrong. I held this until Mrs. Chillingworth's eldest son left school. I then left for him to go on with the management, with the help of a working foreman. I gained experience there. We kept a good flock of sheep, and used to plough with a team of oxen. We then fatted the oxen after two or three years' work from them, and broke in others to take their place. I had the use of the horse and trap to go to Reading Market, sold the corn, and did, I might say, her business in full, and the best part of it was Mrs. Chillingworth seemed satisfied. I kept up their acquaintance for years after I left them—in fact, I do so with her youngest son up to the present time.

CHAPTER X.

MY FIRST TWO FARMS.

After I left Bradfield I went to stay with my sister and brother-in-law, Mr. James Randall, at Stratfieldsaye. I used to attend the Church there, and soon got acquainted with the Rector (the Rev. Gerald Joyce) and Mrs. Joyce. In June, 1857, Mr. Joyce came to me and asked if I would take a situation. I said I would if I could hear of something suitable. He then told me that Mrs. Brocas, of Beaurepaire, was wanting someone to look after her estate, and he thought I should do for it. I might say that Mrs. Joyce was niece to Mrs. Brocas. They, I believe, went to Beaurepaire, and spoke to Mrs. Brocas about the matter, and came to me and asked me if I would go and meet Mrs. Brocas's brother (Rev. Henry Barker), Mr. Juppy (her lawyer), and himself, on a certain morning at Beaurepaire. I at first rather hesitated, having in my mind at the time that I would rather get back into Berkshire again, as I had got on well there for the last six or seven years. But, however, Mr. Joyce wished me to go and meet these gentlemen and hear what they had to say. I did so, and the meeting was very pleasant. I was granted everything I asked, so of course, I could not do otherwise than take it up. The terms agreed upon were for me to spend three

days a week looking over the estate and to keep on
with my brother-in-law, thinking he would not like my
leaving him at once. This went on for a time,
then Mrs. Brocas wished me to come and live in
her house. She allowed me the Steward's room
downstairs for a living and sitting room and a
bedroom on the first floor, and a room at the
gardener's cottage for an office. This all went well
for a time. The next change was that she had given
her tenant at Lodge Farm (which was just at the
back of her house adjoining the shrubbery) notice
to leave, and she would like me to take it on my
own account as it would make my remuneration
better. I could manage the farm and look after
the estate as well. I could keep my rooms and live
in her house until such time as I could get the
farm house ready and furnished. I had to say to
Mrs. Brocas I did not think I could take the farm,
as I had not sufficient capital. I possessed, all told,
about £304, and the farm was 230 acres, the rent
£230, and the tithe about £60. For this reason I
could not venture upon it for two or three months.
She, however, wished me to have it, or otherwise I
must let it. I had applications made for it. I at
last went into Basingstoke and asked Mr. William
Forder Smith, who seemed to be a friend to everybody, if he would lend me some money as I wanted
to take a farm, but had not money enough. He
asked me how much I wanted, so I told him £200,
and he wrote me out a cheque at once. I gave him

a note of hand at five per cent. I came back and agreed to have the farm with my capital of £304, and the £200 borrowed. After two years I took the borrowed capital back to Mr. Smith. He said he was surprised at my bringing it back so soon. I told him that I thought it was always the best way to pay off as soon as one had got the money.

When I first took this farm the road leading to it was out of the new road through the upper end of Pepperwood Coppice, but while I was occupying the farm I grubbed nearly two acres of the coppice and made the road good, planted quick-set hedges on both sides, which much improved the approach to the farm. I used to meet Mr. W. W. Chute often strolling round that way, looking round his Estate. He would generally stop and talk. He seemed to give me encouragement for what I was doing. I did altogether a good deal of grubbing while I had the farm. A big, wide old lane used to pass through the farm. I grubbed that and added it to the farm, and improved it as much as I could during the six years I held it, and my capital increased a hundred a year. During the time I was living at Beaurepaire Farm, the Root Show was started at Basingstoke, when Mr. Henry Downs, auctioneer and land valuer, was a prominent man there; and he, with Mr. Chute, of the Vyne, Mr. Beach, Oakley Hall, and many other landlords and tenant-farmers — myself among others — first began with a root show. After that had been carried on for a year or two we commenced to hold a cattle show. Landlords and tenants held together and got up a fairly good local cattle show called the Basingstoke Show, which was at first held on Thursday in Whitsun week, and was fixed for that day for the first few years. It has now grown to a great magnitude and is called the Royal Counties Agricultural Show. I don't know if there is anyone living but myself that had to do with, and helped to start from the beginning, this important show. There were at that time some very excellent farmers in the neighbourhood of Basingstoke—the Bartons, the Budds, the Clifts at Sherborne and Swallick, besides the Butlers, Tubbs, Randall and Clifts here in these parts, the Cobdens, Reeds, Parkers, Portsmouths, Barretts, Curtises, Huttons, Moody, and many others. Nowhere wherever I travelled did I see better flocks and better farming. The flocks of ewes and sheep were large and numerous, and I don't think it would be any exaggeration to say that as many thousands were kept then as there are hundreds now, and I am sure both landlords and tenants highly respected each other. There were at that time some of the good old-fashioned gentry as landowners. About this time I began to claim a vote for Members of Parliament. I gave my first votes to Mr. Beach and Mr. Sclater-Booth : this was before the old divisions of North Hants and South Hants were split up into their present constituencies. After the division I voted for Mr. Sclater-Booth, then for

Mr. Jeffreys. I always voted Conservative, and I am proud to say that I never had any occasion to alter my opinion. All these M.P.'s distinguished themselves highly in their various official positions.

Mrs. Brocas once asked me if I should like to see over the Houses of Parliament, and told me if I would she would get me a permit. I accepted, and a permit was sent me signed by the Earl of Ducie. It came about in this way. Mr. John Raymond Barker, of Fairford Park, Gloucestershire, Mrs. Brocas' brother, whom I occasionally used to see at Beaurepaire, married as his second wife the daughter of the Earl of Ducie, and the permit came at his request.

I recall a little incident that occurred at the time I was with Mrs. Brocas. A difference of opinion arose between us once in settling some business matter. As it stood, in my view it was £20 in my favour. In her view it was not so. After a little talk I yielded to her view and said I was wrong. That settled the matter very quietly. A short time afterwards she gave me the amount. It seemed I was not to be disappointed.

The first big job I had put into my hands to do on the Beaurepaire Estate was to mark and measure £2000 worth of timber, to be put up for sale by auction. To do this Mr. Joyce got the assistance of the Duke of Wellington's woodman from Wolverton, a Mr. Baverstock, who went with me

to see that it was done properly. I had learnt how
to measure timber before this, when I was at
Grazeley. There was a large fall of timber while
I was there, and I used to get with the man that
had to see to it and measure it, and got to learn
how to measure timber by the sliding rule. After
being shown I soon got hold of it, and after the
man came and measured the timber he left the
measurement rased on the butt of each tree. After he
was gone home of a night I used to go round with
my sliding rule and Hopkins' ready-reckoner to see if
I could measure the same trees to make them come to
the same measurement as he did. This I satisfied
myself in doing.

Then the two farms, Stocks and Church
Farms, through the death of a widow, Mrs. Parsons,
were to be re-let. Mrs. Brocas asked me if I could
take them, and expressed a wish that I should do
so, it having been (as she said) in the Clift family
so many years before. The two farms together were
a little over 500 acres. She asked me to get a tenant
for the Beaurepaire Farm, which I did at the same
rent as I had been paying ; and a very good tenant
he was. I then asked to be allowed to take a partner
to help me to take these two farms at Bramley. This
was granted. I then took up my £1100 at Beaurepaire Farm and brought it down to Stocks ; this
was in 1864. James Randall, my brother-in-law,
wished to be my partner. He found me such addi-
tional money and stock as I wanted for the taking

of the two farms, his share being altogether about
£900. This left me the partner with the biggest
share, but, however, I got into the two farms with
about £1800. I was the sole and absolute manager.
The farms had got low and out of condition. We
held it in partnership for four years. I then
thought of getting married. I wanted to dissolve
the partnership, and I offered to pay him out or
he should pay me out, but he seemed to want to
go on with it. Before this could be settled we had
to consult Mrs. Brocas, whether she would take him
or me as tenant. She at once decided the question
and said as I had her Estate to look after I was
to have the farms. The next to be done by us
was to get two valuers, one each, to value the crops,
stock and tillages between us. This was in 1868,
a very dry year. The sum total of the valuation
was £3764 5s 1d; just double what it cost us
to go in. The half share I was called upon to
pay was £1882 2s 6½d. I have the statement
by me now. I paid my partner no interest nor
took any for myself during the four years of
partnership, but out of the business paid the household expenses only. But the capital just about
doubled in the time it was held in partnership.
It was a great satisfaction to me to feel that I had
not lost my partner's money, but on the other hand
gave him an increase upon his investment at the rate
of one hundred per cent. I paid my partner his
share in three instalments, as directed by the

valuers—Messrs. H. Downs and H. E. Raynbird.

When I first came down here to live the public could not put on nor take off goods on the Railway. There was a siding put in when the railroad was made. I think, by an agreement, the siding was made first for the use of the Beaurepaire Estate for heavy goods, such as coals or other goods of that kind. When the neighbouring gentry wanted coals the Company would not stop them here unless they got a permit from Mrs. Brocas. So that if Mr. Chute, at the Vyne, or Mr. Stane, of Sherfield Manor, or any other gentlemen wanted to have anything stopped at the siding, they were obliged to get permission of Mrs. Brocas.

When I got here to live I was often wanting to use the siding to take away my farm produce and to bring other things back. Other people living in the neighbourhood were wanting the same privilege. We then got a petition drawn up and signed, and the Duke of Wellington headed the list, although he said it would not be of much service to him, as he was rather nearer Mortimer than Bramley. In our petition we asked for a Station and goods-yard. We got one of the Directors (Mr. Simonds, of Reading, the head of the brewery firm there), and the traffic manager at Reading to come and see the spot and look round the district and form their own opinion. Mrs. Brocas gave them a day's shooting for their trouble of coming, which pleased them both. I myself used to shoot then for Mrs. Brocas, and I had the pleasure of taking them round, and afterwards left them at Beaurepaire House for Mrs. Brocas to talk the matter over with them. As soon as we got our petition well filled with signatures with the promise of the support of these two gentlemen, we sent it up to the Board of Directors at Paddington, and the issue of it was that they would give us an open siding and goods yard for all heavy traffic, but could not see their way clear to give us a passenger station at that time. Mr. Simonds then told me not to give up at this but let it rest a little while, then try it again. This we did, and found our heavy traffic increased a good deal, although the Company did not give us a Bramley freightage, but our goods were all invoiced to Basingstoke and charged Basingstoke rates. Then after a few years, when we were doing a good amount of heavy traffic but had only a man in charge of the gate to see the goods off and on, and with the traffic increasing daily, we thought it would be as well to petition the Company again for the passenger station. We called a meeting at Bramley Schoolroom, which was well attended by most of the influential gentry in the district. We did not succeed this time. We then thought our failure was through not having someone at the Board of Directors to see that it was properly represented. The matter lay quiet for a few years longer, and then it was taken up again by Mr. Joseph Jibb, who signed himself as " Footsore " from this parish. He hit upon the right thing, and I believe, got our late M.P., Mr. Jeffreys, to present his petition, and succeeded. Mr. Jibb, like the worthiest of Scotchmen, took care of his earnings, and soon got a new house built for himself, wife, and family to live in within a few yards of the Station. I have never heard of his being "footsore" since.

The farming, as far as I can remember, all went on very well with me, with its ups and downs such as we generally get. But I mustn't complain, for in January, 1870, I was blessed with a daughter. Upon this I had congratulations from both my landlady (Mrs. Brocas), and her daughter, and in due course I gave her the name of Sophia Anne. This was the name of a cousin of mine, and my mother's name was Ann. Miss Brocas asked me if I would like her to be sponsor. I told her that I should. Sophia Anne happened to be Mrs. Brocas's name, and also Miss Brocas's. After this, when seeing an old uncle of mine who came to see me, I told him of this incident. Oh, he said, old Madam Brocas, as he used to call her, stood godmother to your Aunt Harriett. That occurred I found afterwards, at this house in 1819. This Mrs. Harriett Brocas lived at Wokefield, and I've heard of their having an Armoury Room there, and believe that most or all of the last family were born there. Their eldest son and heir to this estate was just about my age (born in the end of November, 1827, I was born February 27th, 1828). Mrs.

Harriett Brocas occupied Beaurepaire at the same period. I have heard of her travelling from there to here by coach, drawn by four black horses, and running footmen, and it took them a day to get from Wokefield to Beaurepaire, the roads being so bad. Wokefield was sold to Mr. Robert Allfrey about the year 1840. I believe the Brocas family owned property up till that time from Burghfield Hill to Basingstoke. The last Squire, who should have been the owner of this estate now, I believe, got into connection with some Jews in London and got a mortgage on this estate, and about the year 1870 or thereabouts the mortgage was called in. The reversion of the estate was sold by public auction at Tokenhouse Yard. I went to see it sold, and a a Mr. Allington bought Beaurepaire and Mr. Benyon, of Englefield, bought the Brocas lands portion at Mortimer West End. Mr. Allington, who was from Letchworth Hall, was an invalid and did not live long after he bought it. This reversion being sold did not interfere with Mrs. Brocas's possession. This she held as long as she lived. After the sale of the reversion she told me that she would give me a 21 years' lease of my holdings, which was the utmost power she had, that I might peaceably and uninterruptedly enjoy my tenure after I was no longer her tenant.

Mrs. Brocas did not live long afterwards and Mr. Allington came into possession. I found him an excellent landlord, but he did not live long. It was left by him to a nephew of his, much in minority, so I had for my landlord a Mr. Julius Allington, the father to the heir. This proved a great benefit to me. He and his agent, a Mr. Lindsell, from Hitchin, came a few times to see me and we got on excellent terms. I had begun draining the farm while I was tenant under Mrs. Brocas. We had a brick and tile kiln on the Brocas lands Farm. I used to get tiles from there free and paid the expense of labour myself up till this time. I then asked Mr. Allington if he would let me go on with the work. He agreed to it, if I would pay 5 per cent. for what money he expended. I agreed to this. So I went on and drained the Farms; nearly the whole of it. The money I had laid out and deducted from my half-year's rents while it was being done, amounted to a total of about £650. I was then to give Mr. Allington five pounds as an acknowledgment of our agreement. He never asked me for any more after that and said that he thought the farming was not good enough to pay more. This was in 1878. Then in 1879 there came a very bad season. Mr. Lindsell came up to me and asked me how I was getting on. I told him as well as I could, but made no complaint. He said it was pretty bad times for farmers in his country, in the neighbourhood of Hitchin. He proposed a walk round the farm to see for himself, and after doing so, he came into the house and said to me " Now I want you to keep up your farm in

every way as well as I see it to-day, and we
shall be prepared to help you." He then asked me
if I had overdrawn at the Bank, and I told him I
had not. He said that he was glad to hear that,
for the farmers could not say that in his part.
He had something to do with the Bank at Hitchin;
his wife was a banker's daughter. His next words
were "Don't overdraw your banking account to pay
us; pay everybody else first, and give us what you
can spare." The few I told this to said that they
never heard of such words said to a tenant before.
It was certainly very encouraging to me, when the
next half-year's rent being due, he wrote up to say
"Collect the other few tenants' rents, and send us
what you can spare of your own." My half-year's
rent was £300, and I sent £200, and in due course
had back a full receipt to show that I was not a
defaulter. When the next half-year came the same
notice came again and I did the same as before,
for which I had my full receipt. This kept on, and
I was never asked for more. After the bad times
were gone over, and I felt myself quite able to pay
the full rent, the same message came, but I sent
the full rent (£300). Perhaps this surprised them
—at any rate, they sent me back a cheque for £30
as a present. I was at the time, and have been
ever since, glad to think that I took this step without
having to be asked for it. Although comparative
strangers to me they were excellent landlords.

Then, after a while, they sold the estate to

Messrs. H. and A. Welch Thornton. Mr. Lindsell
invited us (the tenantry) to a champagne dinner at
the Red Lion Inn, Basingstoke, to finish up with us.
He told me at last if I did not get on with my
new landlords, to come to him, and he would let me
have a good farm, better than I had got here.   That
was about 1883 or 1884.   After the Mr. Thorntons
bought it I became their tenant for the remaining
part of my twenty-one years' lease, which terminated
in 1889.   Altogether I got on very well with the Mr.
Thorntons.   I found out how to please them, and
that was to pay them when I was asked, which I
did.   The way I was told when it was required was
this: After coming out of Church on a Sunday
morning, where we generally used to meet, we would
exchange greetings, and then Mr. Alfred would say
"I say, old friend, I wish you would come up to-
morrow morning and bring that old cheque book of
yours with you." Of course I did so, but it seemed
almost painful to see Mr. Thornton's countenance
looking so dejected, as he would say he did not like
taking my money, but supposed he must. As soon
as the receipt was handed to me the liqueur and
whiskey bottles were soon brought on the table to
cheer us both up. After this I knew pretty well how
to please Mr. Thornton, and he would muster up
courage enough to say that he wished it was a little
more.   Here I must not forget to say that I have
spent many happy times with the Mr. and Mrs. Thorn-

tons. I believe I can safely say that I never failed to keep up my payments with any landlord or landlady, and that I never went grumbling nor complaining to them, as I seemed to get what I wanted without that. During the time of my being a tenant farmer (45 years), I have had eight landlords and one landlady. That was Mrs. Brocas first, then two Mr. Allingtons, three Mr. Thorntons and, for Holly Cross, three Dukes of Wellington. I must and am bound to say of them all, that I found them excellent to rent under, and I look back upon the past with much pleasure, and shall be ever thankful to good Mrs. Brocas for her confidence shown in me, which enabled me to make a start.

I first went to the Vyne House in the year 1838. The way we got to the Vyne was quite different then from what it is now. We turned into a road just opposite to the Beaurepaire Lodge and went along over a bridge near the fish pond. This led up to the front of the house. I believe that was then a public road, but not having seen the Vyne House before I did not know how the road continued on to Sherborne.

Mr. William Lide Wiggett Chute was the owner of the Vyne House about the time I was living at Beaurepaire Farm, and I used often to come in contact with him. When he came into the estate he made great alterations and improvements. He altered the road commencing near the Vyne Lodge

Farm and carried it along by the gardener's house and the large oak (the king of oaks, I might say) to the Vyne Farm, and after this the public discontinued the use of the road by the House. A story was told years ago about this old king oak. A timber merchant came one day to the Mr. Chute who owned the estate at that time to buy this oak. The merchant tried a long while, but could not succeed in making a bargain, as the Squire asked £10 more than he would give, so the tree was not sold. The dealer came back the next day and offered £10 more, but the Squire said "No. If the tree will grow £10 in value in one night, I will keep it longer." The Squire went on draining the land where necessary, grubbing and straightening the fences, repairing existing cottages, and building many new ones. All this work was done very substantially and well.

Mr. Chute was a good landlord. He was truly one of the fine old English gentlemen, and was highly respected by all who lived around him. He would help the young and consider the old. I was often meeting him humming a tune and swinging his stick in his hand, and I had ample opportunity of well knowing him. Mr. Chaloner Chute, after he left school, started a cricket club, and got his father, the Squire, to lay out a piece of ground and prepare a cricket pitch, and it is now the present cricket ground. We were all asked to join the cricket club. A very good club was established, and in time some good

matches were played. Mr. Chaloner having so many
cricketing school fellows, and knowing many others,
used to get them here to play. He brought one
club here called the Zingari Club. This match always
excited a good deal of interest. The old Squire, with
Mrs. Chute and family, nearly always came to see
the matches. The ladies brought their needlework,
if it was fine, and sat about on the grass and
watched the match. Sometimes the old Squire would
play in a match. When this happened and he made
a score the ladies would all clap their hands, and
Mrs. Chute would call out " Well done ! William."
The cricket season was finished about the end of
September with a wind up match and a supper at
the Swan Inn, when the chair was taken by the old
Squire and a very pleasant evening used to be spent.

The next thing to be thought of was something
in the way of amusement for the winter evenings.
There was generally one entertainment, and sometimes
two, at the Vyne House during the year. These
took place in the Sculpture-room, I think it was
called, at the south end of the house. I don't think
I ever missed receiving an invitation, except at the
Rent Audit dinners. Then there was another thing.
Mrs. Buckworth, the Rector's wife, who was the
choirmistress, would be asking a host of us to
come to the Rectory once a week or so to
practise singing. In this the parish was pretty
strong ; what with the Hunts (five or six of

them), the Whistlers, the Whites, the Matthews, myself and a few others, we made a good muster, and Mrs. Buckworth, who was well up to her work, could keep all going merrily.

About the year 1860 the North Hants Choral Union was started. Mrs. Buckworth with her choir joined it, and we met once a week for practice. We numbered, I think, all told, about twenty-four. The first festival was held at Church Oakley. The Oakley choir came down to us to have a practice together one evening before it took place. Among them was a gentleman whom I did not know. He was lame at the time, and had a crutch. What struck me so much was that although he was a perfect gentleman he was so delightfully free in his manner, and so friendly with every one of the party, having a smile and a kindly word for everybody. I ultimately found out that it was Mr. William Spencer Portal, of Malshanger. I met him many and many a time after this on similar occasions, and he was always the same as I found him that evening. There was a festival held every year afterwards, either in Basingstoke or some neighbouring Parish Church which was large enough, and once in four years it took place at Winchester Cathedral, where there was a very large gathering. The Isle of Wight and South Hants choirs used to join us there. I think I may safely say that I met Mr. Portal on these occasions for upwards of twenty years after this without a break. I may also say how very bright and interesting to us his speeches were at the dinner table, when it was over. It might be interesting to state that I am now practising with our choir (which began nearly fifty years ago) for the 1909 Festival.

CHAPTER XI.

SOME LATER FARMING EXPERIENCES.

I took the Holly Cross and Barefoots Farms in 1874. I may say here that I believe the right name for this farm is Holly Cross—not Hollow Cross. There was a large holly tree in a field near the house when I was a boy and the farm was then always called Holly Cross. My two eldest brothers, Thomas and Daniel, after the death of my father, went on with these farms, and kept them for their homes for about thirteen years, when they were sold out—but not by the landlord. I went and saw Mr. Mousley (the then Duke's steward) and told him that I would take it and keep it in the family if the Duke had no objection. I very soon had the reply that I might go on with it at once. I was very glad of the opportunity of keeping my birthplace in hand for my family, if they should live to grow up (my sons were very young then). The object sought for soon came, as after I had occupied it for about a year (or hardly so much), I had a younger brother, who left home and went to London for a few years, and wished to come back in the country again. He did not save much money, although he was in the Agra Bank, Nicholas Lane. I took him as a partner, thinking that he would after a time be able to save

enough money to pay me off and make it his own.
But it did not prove so. It was carried on in
partnership for eight or nine years, and I found
that he kept getting further behind in his payments. I was obliged then to take the matter up
and thoroughly go into it, and I found it worse
than I expected. I then paid him all the money
he put into the business (less fifty pounds), and I
took the debts to clear off, which cost me nearly as
much as it did at my first taking the farm.

It is all very well to have money I'll own,

    But to do a good turn when you can

And put your shoulder to the wheel,

    'Tis a motto for every man.

This I had to do, and fortunately I had "Ball in the
stable." [This old saying means having a reserve for
cases of emergency]. After this I kept it in my own
hands for a few years and placed my eldest son in
it. After he had been farming a few years, my
second son, after serving two years in Tasker and
Sons' Foundry at Andover, then wanted to do
something for himself. Mr. Clift, my relation, of
Manor Farm, Sherborne St. John, gave up his farm,
and it was in the market for some few months. It
came into my head one night, when on the pillow,
that I would go and see if I could take it, and I
at once succeeded in doing so. I then sent Ernest
W. B. to that farm, and sent William G., my
second son, into Holly Cross, Barefoots, and Hyde-

house Farms. There was in times gone by a Jesse Barefoot Clift, from whom, no doubt, the farm took its name. The last generation had let the name drop out of the family, but I thought that I would pick it up again. The name of William Clift first appears in my family register in 1673. As far as I can find out I am the fifth William Clift in descent, and fifth William occupier of this house. It seems singular to me to state that all the lands that the Clift families have ever owned or occupied in this parish have come into my hands to farm and occupy, excepting Oliver's Farm, occupied by my father for one year. How very unforeseen things occur in one's life! I must say—"Never despise the day of small things"; for I am able to say that my start in life was the buying of three chicken at a shilling apiece of old Mrs. Keep, living in an old thatched cottage near Herrett's Farm, Strathfieldsaye, one night when going home from school. These I kept and sold at 2s. 6d. each. I had then 7s. 6d. to put in my pocket. After that I bought eight more of the same Mrs. Keep. I kept them and sold them at 2s. 6d. each. This brought me the first sovereign I ever had of my own. I kept on investing my money in young goslings and chickens. I used to go to Newnham Common, where there were a lot of goslings bred. I bought them when two or three weeks old at about 1s. 2d. or 1s. 3d. each. A sovereign went a good way in buying young things.

It used to give me employment in looking after them ; and at Christmas I could make 12s. or 14s. apiece for the geese.   I kept them until Christmas because they produced so many more feathers then, and they also produced a lot of down under the feathers, which they did not have if they were killed and picked at Michaelmas.   Down does not come up on a goose until after Michaelmas.   The feathers were picked and kept by themselves, the down being separated from it, put into bags and placed in a warm brick oven to get them thoroughly dry.   Then they were put away in a dry room ready to be looked over by hand, the feathers being used for making beds, and the down for making pillows.   I think the only fortune my father could afford to give his ten children when they left home was a good feather bed each, and I must say what a very comfortable one it was.   I immensely enjoy mine every night at the present time, and thankful I am for being able to do so after I have finished my long clay pipe and glass of grog, for this was my father's custom, and so it shall be mine.

The only fuel used in villages was wood.   In my father's house there was not used a ton of coal in a year in my early days.   We used to enjoy the wood fires and the Yule logs, sitting in the roomy chimney corners of the large open fire-places.   In winter time the children took their meals in their cosy corners, their laps being their only table ; while for the parents, and, perhaps, the elder children, a table

was brought close up to the great wood fire. No
coal could be got except from the towns or from
some coal depôt or wharf by a navigable river or
canal, along which barges plied : and with roads so
bad, and distances so great, coal became very
costly by the time it could reach the villages. But
we were blessed with plenty of good wood growing
around us, and it may be relied upon that we did
not always sit cold.

My brother Thomas once said to James King
(one of the workmen on the farm) that he should
like to live long enough to see what Master Billie
would come to. This was told me by James King
after I had taken possession of their two farms.
My brother Thomas did not live to see that, but
my brother Daniel did.

I took these farms in a perfectly bare condition ;
everything on them was sold by auction—hay, straw,
roots, caving, &c. I never could understand how this
came to be allowed by the then Duke's steward, and
why the auctioneer was not stopped from selling as
soon as the amount claimed was realised. In taking
the farms I had to find for my use all the hay and
straw I required for the first year, but after this Mr.
Mousley and I made this matter right. I did a great
deal of work to the farms during the time I had
them in my own hands. I had new wells dug (one
in each yard) and pumps and troughs put up for the
horses and cattle, instead of taking them into dirty

ponds for water. I got a new stable and cowsheds at Holly Cross, drained some of the fields, grubbed hedgerows, made roads, &c., filled up the bottoms of the yards, made additions to the house and built an outhouse.

The house at Holly Cross was built new in 1798. About that time, I was told, the granary, now standing beside the road at Holly Cross, was taken down from Barefoot's Farm and put there whole. Some people wondered how this could be done, but I don't think there was much difficulty about a job like that. The lanes then were nothing but mud and dirt, and I believe the granary was moved by putting skids under it and drawing it along on the mud with horses. After this the news got about that the well was to be moved from one side of the house to the other ; and one old farmer, whose favourite expression was "Dimme soul, boy," said to his people at home "dimme soul" if he wouldn't go and see this well moved down at Farmer Clift's, taken out whole, as he thought, and put round the other side of the house! When he got to Bramley he found that the old well was only domed over and a new one dug at the other side of the house. The people all laughed at him for his simplicity, and cut his initials (C.T., 1798) on a brick in the wall, and it is to be seen there now. The same farmer—Charles Tubb—'twas once said, went down to his boy who was at harrow in his field one day. He found the boy lying down and not at work. When he got to him he said "Dimme soul,

boy, if you don't get up I'll knock'ee down." Farmer
Tubb after this was called "Dimme soul, boy."

I must now say something about my career as a
tenant farmer. I began in 1858 at Beaurepaire Farm
with

> Two old chairs and a table—
> That we called a pair ;
> And outside the door a stable
> To lodge the old grey mare.

Business went on pretty well, with a step upwards in
most years as they followed. If I had reverses, which
I think most people have to deal with occasionally, I
forgot them as soon as I could and dwelt more on
the better years when they came along, and I think
now it is the best thing to do, for when anything
happens which you cannot prevent, it is wisest to
pass on as if nothing had happened. In 1860
farming looked very deplorable ; it was an extremely
wet year, and I remember sitting indoors for two
whole days together reading "The Scottish Chiefs,"
the rain falling incessantly the whole time. The
wheat was then just fit to cut. I went into Basingstoke on the evening of the second day and met
farmers coming in and saying that their wheat was
growing out in the ear as it stood—it had got so
ripe and wanted cutting. Mine was not so bad as
that, for I don't think I had any grown out. At
the end of the week the weather took up fine, and
continued so the whole of the harvest. I began
cutting wheat on the 5th of September, and had a

good crop. I think I am right in saying it made sixty-two and sixty-three shillings per quarter for the whole of that year. I also had a good crop of barley, harvested well, which made two guineas per quarter, as well as a good crop of beans, which I finished carrying on the 22nd November. I had also two good crops of clover hay that year, and old Mr. Goffe, of Basing, came over and brought a London hay-buyer with him, who bought the whole and gave me £5 per ton for it, and this was in November. Beans were a fairly good crop, but we could not get them very dry. I remember selling some for seed in the following spring at £2 per quarter. I happened to find a good customer, or I should not have made so much.

The year 1860 looked ruinous in September, but it proved a money saving year for me, and I put "Ball in the stable" that year, and went on my way rejoicing. I held Beaurepaire Farm for four years after this, but kept an eye on my old grey mare in the stable. She, having carried me safely through this expected bad year, ought not to be forgotten in case another bad year might come. In 1864 Mrs. Brocas wished me to come down to the Stocks, which I did, after I had found her a suitable tenant for Beaurepaire Farm.

I came here to live in 1865 and took in a partner by Mrs. Brocas' consent, to enable me to work the farm. The rent was £500 a

year, and the tithes, which were nearly £200 more
a year. After the partnership betwixt me and Mr.
Randall was dissolved, and I got a good deal of the
land drained and some grubbing done, Mrs. Brocas
wanted another £100 a year, and she would give
me a twenty-one years' lease of the farm, so
that I might peaceably and uninterruptedly enjoy my
occupation after her death. I accepted the farm on
these conditions, but it would not have been of the
service to me that it was had I not been fortunate
in having good landlords after Mrs. Brocas had gone.

The length of time I held land as a tenant
farmer was forty-five years. I had in my hands during
that time something over a thousand acres (though not
all at one time), and I calculate that the amount of
money that came into my hands and was paid by me
as rent, tithes, labour, poor rates, taxes, upkeep of
my house, tradesmen's bills, etc., amounted in the
aggregate to over one hundred thousand pounds. I
believe the holding that I have had in hand to farm
was formerly held by twelve different occupiers a
century ago. My object in writing this is to give
some idea of what a large holding is capable of
returning by the management of one occupant. As
there is a great deal said at the present time about
putting land back into small holdings, if anyone
reading this would like to take the matter up for
discussion as to which is the best for the community
and for the circulation of money—small holdings or

large — they are welcome to this record of my experience. I myself should like to see more tenant farmers as occupiers of the land, but I do like to see also the land well managed. Having been bred as a tiller of the soil, and my forefathers also for generations back, there is no wonder at my holding up this as the highest and noblest of callings.

> Samson was the strongest man ;
> Solomon was the wisest ;
> Alexander for to conquer
> Was his daily pride ;
> King David was a valiant man,

ERRATUM.

For the word "servants," line 19, page 111, read "tenants."

And their ~~servants~~ ne'er fail.

I have found Mother Earth to be the best of all friends. "The better you treat your friends the better your friends treat you," and the better one treats the soil the more remuneration it returns. One of my father's instructions to me was "Whatever is worth doing at all is worth doing well." Another matter which he was always very strict about was "A place for everything, and everything in its place." The keys of all barns, granaries, and storehouses that were usually locked up at night had to be brought into the house and hung up on a certain nail, so that one could go and get them in the dark if required. The same rule was also enforced with regard to the tools used in our daily work.

I must now bring my reminiscences to a close. I don't think I should ever have put them into print had I not been prompted and asked so to do by His Grace the Duke of Wellington. All that I now wish to say is that they are correct statements to the best of my recollection. Should there be anything in them that will be found of interest and worth reading by His Grace or any others who by chance see this book, I shall feel myself well rewarded for what I have done.

It is curious to notice the recurrence of the figure 8 in the memorable events of my life. Thus :—

Born 1828

Became Choirboy in Bramley Church 1838

Left home to go into service ... 1848

Took Beaurepaire Farm on my own account 1858

Married 1868

Finished draining Stocks, Church, and Minchin's Farms (grubbing up 41 hedgerows thereon at my own expense) 1878

Took Interest on £1000 4 per cent. New Zealand Stock 1888

Was able to say that I had rented under eight landlords 1898

Wrote these reminiscences 1908

This Chapter was written subsequently to the rest of the book at my request in order to show the author's opinion on the subject of Small Holdings.—
WELLINGTON.

CHAPTER XII.

THE CHANGE FROM THE SMALL TO THE LARGE FARMS.

I go on to write a little about the small owners of land in the past. My own knowledge of some of them, and what has been told me of many others, shows that in former days, when a little money was made, as soon as it could be spared, it was invested in land. Money was scarce in those days ; but then, as now, there were always some who saved and some who did not. Besides, the chance of advantageous investment, with good security, was not then so easily got. So investment of money in land was held to be the safest ; and I used to hear them say that the money was invested in safety, for the land could not run away. But some found out that though the land could not run away, its realisable value could. I have known many well-to-do men who took the same view of the stability of land investments, and invested largely in the purchase of land, but they could not realise without a loss. A farmer owning from 50 to 100 acres would get himself a homestead put up for his own accommodation without spending much money on the buildings, for the farms generally being in small fields and heavily timbered, they had hardly any material to buy, wood and thatch being the chief materials used in cottages as well as farm buildings. In course of years these buildings became dilapidated, and probably were so when the family of the first owner eventually desired to share the property amongst them. The general course taken was to sell the property for cash, so that the money could be divided.

These small farms could do no more than keep the family. They produced nearly all the family wanted to live on. Every implement that was used was made of home-grown timber, and made by the local carpenter, smith, or wheelwright. After the farmers discontinued growing hops there was not much they grew that they could realise money from. I have every reason to believe that my ancestors became possessed of their land before the last century — in the seventeen hundreds. I have ascertained that there were several fields owned by them then. What a change from then till now! As I have said before, I would rather be a tenant than an owner now. There must have been a good many hops grown at that time. This is certain, because so many fields are still called "hop gardens." The old hop kilns were standing in my early days. Judging from the experience of my own family, I think farming was very good at that time, but became worse after the hop growing was discontinued. The wheat crop was the chief stay to the farmer : there was not much besides, except the beans, that could be spared to turn into money ; and even the beans were required, in part, for feeding purposes. Peas and barley crops were used for feeding pigs — the bacon to be used in the house, for the consumption of food was large. Carters, boys, and all men employed looking after cattle, were fed in the house. They came in three times a day—first to breakfast on bread, bacon, bread and milk, and coffee ; lunch, consisting of bread and cheese, with a bottle of small beer, was eaten in the field ; when they came home at 3 o'clock, their meal consisted of plain pudding, bacon and vegetables ; and before going to bed in the evening, they had bread and cheese, with beer. So that most of the produce of a small farm really went to keep the house going. This food was given to the labourers as part payment for their work ; they had but little money besides their rations. And for such times, such customs were very suitable.

I have a map of the Stocks Farm, dated 1762, which shows how many small owners there were. The total acreage of this farm was 238 acres, but scattered about it were several fields, owned by different people.

My memory bears me back to the years 1832-3, and I remember seeing at that time many old dilapidated buildings, barns, and stables standing without tenants. There were, it seemed, no tenants to be found for them, and the owners did not want to farm their land themselves. So these old buildings on the small farms were pulled down, and the land, of necessity, laid to the adjoining farm by amicable arrangement between tenant and landlord. As farming was not good in those days, and landlords did not want the farms on their own hands, the farms became larger by the small farm being added to the larger one, and any material in the old buildings which was still of use went to make better accommodation for the increased necessities of the larger farm. I have known five or six cases of the sort in this parish of Bramley, and as many in Stratfieldsaye.

After this there came a period of good farming. The farms were enlarged and underground drained by the landlords, and many young farmers started with a vigorous determination to make a do of it, in which they succeeded to my knowledge. The landlords cut the timber, and the tenants grubbed out the hedge-rows and enlarged the fields, chalking them where necessary. Old Mr. Butler, of this parish, had four sons and put them all to farming, and good farmers they were too, and made a fairly good lot of money in a few years. I know of many farmers in the field country that made a good deal of money about this period.

From what I can remember, farming was not very good until towards the end of the thirties, but early in the forties the railways began to come into use, and I saw both the G.W.R. and S.W.R. in process of making. All sorts of farm produce quickly went up in value as the railways gave the farmer the chance of selling his hay, straw and corn at better prices in distant markets. As soon as the railways were opened, there was a great demand for promising young men of good character to take up employment on them, and a great many farmers' sons and others left their homes and entered the railway service at good wages. Six went from this parish; two of my brothers took advantage of the opportunity.

In 1840 the penny post was brought into use, and that drew a great many young men from the country to fill the various positions that were offered. Just about this time also the high wages earned in the coal mines took many families from the country round. Some came back, but many never did. Then came the boom of America with its prairies, and thousands of the English peasantry emigrated from the rural districts, never to return. America took the attention of agricultural workers particularly, and wonderful stories of the possibilities were told, and believed. Well do I remember Russell's song, sung by thousands in England :—

To the West ! To the West ! To the land of the free,
Where the mighty Missouri runs down to the sea,
Where the young may exult, and the aged may rest,
Away, far away, in the land of the West !

Then another draft of our best charactered and most prominent young men was made by the establishment of the Rural Police by Sir Robert Peel. Another industry, the iron foundries, took thousands of the working class; and many other important manufactures were commenced about this time. For instance, the Biscuit Factory at Reading made increased demands upon the workers, until it now employs thousands of hands. I believe that in the latter end of the thirties Mr. Huntley, of the firm of Huntley and Palmer, ran a barrow about Reading with his biscuits for sale! This was told me by some very old friends of mine at the time I was living with them at Grazeley, near Reading.

All these causes have in some measure contributed to take the young men from the country districts, and produce a disinclination for agricultural pursuits, thereby effectually extinguishing the small farmer. The landlords would have retained them if they could; but as times were, the small farmer was bound to become extinct. My own experience of landlords is this: I can truly say that all the landlords with whom I have had dealings have done their duty to me as tenant. And I think the landlords of the surrounding country have done equally well for their tenants, if they were found worthy of it. The land has changed ownership, but the tenancy has been undisturbed, and I may say **peaceably enjoyed.**

There is now more disposition to take land than there was a few years ago. I know of five or six men who within the past few years have taken land, having wisely saved a little money. Two of them now occupy over 200 acres each. They do not go to the County Council to borrow money from the county rates; but do their own business quite to themselves. In my opinion they have begun in the way most likely to enable them to hold their own. I do not think it would be wise to give land into the hands of anyone who has never been in any way accustomed to the management of land, nor brought up on it; and to borrow money to help them in their experiments, would, I fear, not lead to good results. The people who have been brought up in other businesses generally seem to want quicker returns than are made from the land. They do not take into consideration that they can keep their house going the first year by getting a few cows, pigs, and poultry. These, well managed, will do a good deal towards the first year's outgoing. I say this from my own experience. About fifteen years ago in this parish there were a few labouring people who asked for land in small holdings. Our then clergyman (the Rev. C. Eddy) and Mr. Mousley (Steward to the Duke of Wellington) got the Duke to let them have some land. The Steward formed out roads for each of the men to get to their various allotments, and went to some considerable expense to give the men a good start. They kept it as long as they could and got themselves into debt. The land got out of cultivation, and I believe the landlord had to make a sacrifice in some instances and offer it to a better tenant. What few there are remaining of those that first took the land are not doing it as if it would last long. These are my experiences of small allotment holdings.

SONGS SUNG IN THE OLDEN DAYS.

TUBAL CAIN.

Tubal Cain was a man of might
  In the days when earth was young,
By his fierce red light and his furnace bright,
  The strokes of his hammer rung ;
He lifted high his brawny hand
  As the iron was glowing clear,
Till the sparks rushed out in a scarlet rout
  As he fashioned the sword and spear.

  So they sang Hurrah to Tubal Cain,
    Hurrah to his spear and sword,
  Hurrah to the hand that would wield them well,
    For he shall be king and lord.

To Tubal Cain came many a one,
  As he sat by his roaring fire,
And each one prayed for a strong steel blade
  And a crown of his heart's desire.
He made them weapons sharp and strong,
  Their hearts he filled with glee,
He gave them gifts and perels of gold
  And spoils of the forest free.

  So they sang, &c.

THE GIPSY'S TENT.

Our fire on the turf, and tent 'neath the tree,
Carousing by moonlight so merry are we ;
Let the lord boast his castle, the baron his hall,
But the home of a gipsy is widest of all.
We laugh at our cup, and shout loud as we will,
Till echo rings back from woods, welkin and hill ;
There's no joy seems to us like the joys that are
    spent
By a wanderer's life in a gipsy's tent.

> There's no joy seems to us like the joys that
>   are spent
> By a wanderer's life in a gipsy's tent.

Your fancies all beauty, but where will you seek
Such bloom as is found on the tawny-one's cheek ?
Our limbs that move nimbly, and bounding with
    health,
Are worth all your pale faces and coffers of wealth.
We have nought to control us, we list or we loam,
Our will is our law, and the world is our home ;
Ev'n Job wouldn't repine at his lot if he'd spent
A night of wild glee in a gipsy's tent.

> Ev'n Job wouldn't repine at his lot if he'd
>   spent
> A night of wild glee in a gipsy's tent.

Some crime and much folly may fall to our lot,
We have sins, and, pray, where is there one that
    has not ?
We are rogues, arrant rogues, but remember 'tis
    rare

That we take but from those who can very well
  spare.
You may tell us of deeds justly branded with shame,
But if great ones heard truth, we might tell them
  the same ;
For there's many a king would have less to repent
If his throne was as pure as a gipsy's tent.

> For there's many a king would have less to
>   repent
> If his throne was as pure as a gipsy's tent.

THE NAVY AND THE ARMY.

When war no more with ruthless hands
  Spreads gloom and terror round,
Be not forgot that glorious band
  That England's glory crowned.
Then, while the glass you gaily pass,
  Let mirth and music charm ye,
Let Britons' boast be England's toast—
  The Navy and the Army.

> The Navy and the Army,
> The Army and the Navy,
> Let Britons' boast be England's toast,
> The Navy and the Army.

The sailors on the mountain waves,
  The soldiers in the field,
They boldly fight, humanely save,
  But never basely yield.
Then, while the glass you gaily pass,

Let mirth and music charm ye,
Let Britons' boast be England's toast—
The Navy and the Army.

The Navy and the Army,
The Army and the Navy,
Let Britons' boast be England's toast—
The Navy and the Army.

DAME DURDEN.

Dame Durden kept five servant men
To use the spade and flail ;
She also kept five servant maids
To carry the milking pails.
'Twas Moll and Bet, and Doll and Kit,
And Dorothy Draggle-tail ;
And 'twas Bob and Dick, and Jack and Will,
And Humphrey with his flail.

So Bob kissed Bettie,
And Dick kissed Moll,
And Jack kissed Kittie,
And Will kissed Doll ;
Then there was Humphrey with his flail,
But Kittie, she was the charming maid
That carried the milking pail,
But Kittie, she was the charming maid
That carried the milking pail.

Dame Durden in the morn so soon
She did begin to call,
To rouse her servants, maids and men,

So loudly she did bawl.
To Moll and Bet, and Doll and Kit,
　And Dorothy Draggle-tail,
And to Bob and Dick, and Jack and Will,
　And to Humphrey with his flail.
　　　And Bob kissed Mollie,
　　　　And Dick kissed Bet,
　　　And Jack kissed Dollie,
　　　　And Will kissed Kit ;
　　Then there was Humphrey with his flail,
　　But Kittie, she was the charming maid
　　　That carried the milking pail,
　　But Kittie, she was the charming maid
　　　That carried the milking pail.

When in the morn of Valentine,
　And birds began to mate,
Dame Durden, with her maids and men,
　They all began to prate.
There was Moll and Bet, and Doll and Kit,
　And Dorothy Draggle-tail,
And Will and Jack, and Dick and Bob,
　And Humphrey with his flail.
　　　Then Will kissed Bettie,
　　　　And Jack kissed Moll,
　　　And Dick kissed Kittie,
　　　　And Bob kissed Doll ;
　　Then there was Humphrey with his flail,
　　But Kittie, she was the charming maid
　　　That carried the milking pail,
　　But Kittie, she was the charming maid
　　　That carried the milking pail.

HARRY BLUFF.

Harry Bluff when a boy left his friends and his
home,
And his dear native land, on the ocean to roam ;
Like a sapling he sprung, he was fair to the view,
Like a true British oak, boys, the older he grew.
'Tho his body was weak, and his hands they were
soft,
When the signal was given he was first up aloft ;
And the veterans all cried he will one day lead
the van,
'Tho rated a boy, he'd the soul of a man,
  And the heart of a true British sailor.

When in manhood promoted, and burning for fame,
In peace or in war, Harry Bluff was the same ;
He was true to his love, and in battle so brave.
Now the myrtle and laurel entwine o'er his grave.
For his country he fell, when by victory was crowned,
The flag shot away, fell in tatters around ;
The foe thought he was struck, when he sung out
Avast,
And the colours of old England he nailed to the
mast,
  And he died like a true British sailor.

*Sung by Mr. George Foster at the Officers' Club House,
Aldershot, at their dinner at the finish of the season of the
Drag Hounds, 1908.—Captain Harris St. John, 16th Lancers,
Secretary.*

www.ingramcontent.com/pod-product-compliance
Lightning Source LLC
LaVergne TN
LVHW081346060426
835508LV00017B/1436